THE BASICS OF
SPECULATING

Gerald Krefetz

Dearborn
Financial Publishing, Inc.

While a great deal of care has been taken to provide accurate and current information, the ideas, suggestions, general principles and conclusions presented in this text are subject to local, state and federal laws and regulations, court cases and any revisions of same. The reader is thus urged to consult legal counsel regarding any points of law—this publication should not be used as a substitute for competent legal advice.

Publisher: Kathleen A. Welton
Associate Editor: Karen A. Christensen
Senior Project Editor: Jack L. Kiburz
Interior Design: Lucy Jenkins
Cover Design: Sam Concialdi

Published by Dearborn Financial Publishing, Inc.

Printed in the United States of America

92 93 94 10 9 8 7 6 5 4 3 2 1

Library of Congress Cataloging-in-Publication Data

Krefetz, Gerald
     The basics of speculating / Gerald Krefetz.
        p. cm. — (Making the most of your money series)
     Includes index.
     ISBN 0-79310-361-4 (paper)
        1. Speculation. 2. Investments. I. Title. II. Series: Krefetz,
     Gerald. Making the most of your money series.
HG6015.K74 1992   91-42814
332.64'5—dc20   CIP

Dedication

To Dorothy, Nadine and Adriene

Contents

Introduction

IS SPECULATING FOR YOU?

Speculating is clearly not for everyone. People with disposable income are investing (whether or not they think of it in those terms) when they put money in a house, raw land, certificates of deposit, EE savings bonds, tax-free municipals or a money market account. Only by saving in the venerable mattress do they opt out of the investment loop.

Since many people are investing, knowingly or not, are they also speculating? Is speculating a separate activity, or is it part and parcel of investing or a by-product of investing? What are the similarities and differences?

The first thing to consider is that investing and speculating are both the opposite of gambling. Gambling is pure chance or pure risk. Gambling is a game—one worth winning, but it may not be a game worth playing. In other words, it is worthwhile to win the lottery or sweepstakes, but it is hardly worth buying tickets, considering the chances of winning.

While gambling is derived from gaming, speculating is an ancient practice, named after the Roman activity *speculari,* which means "to spy out or watch." It eventually came to mean "looking ahead in business" or "buying and selling commodities to profit by a rise or fall in their market value." One who speculates assumes that some action or event is likely, probable or even certain. If the speculator is to be successful, he or she can profit only by observing, considering or reflecting. It is, in brief, a forward-looking occupation.

Speculating differs from investing in terms of perspective. When an investment is undertaken, there is a heavy weighing of past factors. Working on the theory that a company can do again what it has done before, the investor decides if it is worth paying the price (some multiple of annual earnings) at which a company's stock trades. Thus, if a company's stock has earned $3 per share and has sold, on average, at ten times earnings, a current investment price of around $30 is justified.

However, if the price of a stock is more than the normal multiple, anyone who buys it at that higher price is presumably buying on the expectation of an increase in the earnings. The excess value in the purchase price can be considered the speculative component. The investor is buying future hopes that can be realized only if a company excels. It must exceed what it has done before.

A company must increase its revenues and earnings, and it must increase research and development to come up with exciting new products. In short, it must do what it has not done as yet. This is obviously no easy task—and it is a task that makes a company speculative.

According to this school of thought, an initial public offering for a new company has to be considered speculative since there is no past by which to judge the company. Price then becomes a large determinant of whether an investment is speculative or not.

This raises the question of what, if anything, future earnings are worth. To the hard-nosed investment managers who are accountable to boards, committees and oversight agencies, the answer is *not much*. Decisions are made on past performance, not on future promises. While this approach may satisfy some staid portfolio managers of other people's money, it is somewhat of a disingenuous argument. The stock markets (and the bond markets to a lesser degree) are perennially looking toward future events and developments.

All participants in the securities markets must ask themselves at least two questions before plunging in. The first is, What is the company worth? And what do its assets amount to? This requires appraising the company's record of earnings from its income statement. This includes its revenues; cash flow; and the critical ratios of price, growth, dividends and credit.

If that was all you had to consider, you might well have ended up in the best buggy-whip companies, steam-driven locomotive businesses, transatlantic sailing ships, hand-operated washing machines and manufacturers of radio tubes—all wonderful businesses that lacked foresight and imagination. Thus, it is important to ask a second question: What will the company do to enhance its products, improve its future earnings and increase its successes? Without a vision and a plan (some might even say a "dream"), a business is courting obsolescence. The most conservative investors should not be so skeptical as to forgo projections of future successes.

THE RISK IN SPECULATING

How then do investors and speculators differentiate themselves? Is one person's investment another's speculation? Both appear to consider the same factors, but investors tend to take a longer view and are decidedly more uncomfortable with risk.

Speculators, on the other hand, are not risk-averse. They welcome risk. But this is not to say that they are unconcerned about the investment criteria of safety, rate of return, liquidity and tax status. They have a healthy regard for these factors since their ultimate success is as much dependent on them as it is for investors. But where investors are on guard against risk as represented by future prospects, speculators welcome these prospects and pride themselves on their ability to anticipate them and profit thereby.

Speculators use all their "street smarts" to detect what is about to happen. Their intuition, their contacts and their sense of the markets are all used to bolster their perceptions. What matters to speculators is to arrive at quick, practical assessments of value, devoid of fear, greed, envy, patriotism, morality or public loathing. Speculators have always acted in their own interest, frequently contrary to general sentiment. As a result, they have had a poor reputation throughout history. When economic problems arise—whether caused by political ineptitude, corporate mismanagement, public euphoria or natural disaster—speculators are inevitably blamed. They are denounced because they usually take positions contrary to what governments wish and citizens demand.

Thus, when prices of petroleum rise after an oil spill, speculators are to blame. When prices of cereal grains skyrocket after a summer drought, speculators are to blame. When there is a shortage of anything from pork bellies to semiconductor chips, speculators are to blame.

The arguments that cite speculators and short-term traders as the villains in every economic crisis usually suffer from the fallacy of *post hoc, ergo propter hoc* (after this, therefore on account of this). Crises move speculators to act; speculators do not cause the crises.

Justice Oliver Wendell Holmes remarked that speculation is the "self-adjustment of society to the probable. Its value is well known as a means of avoiding or mitigating catastrophes, equalizing prices and providing for periods of want." Speculators provide a public service in periods of near panic, but the public is rarely thankful when peace and calm return. Thus speculators are castigated for avariciousness, greed and taking advantage when the public is acting only for altruistic reasons.

A healthy dose of self-interest should mark all parties interested in the financial world. However, it is the accommodation to risk that signals the activities of speculators. This tolerance for risk simply means that speculators are willing and prepared to lose capital. To put it slightly differently, the courts have found that any investments made by fiduciaries and trustees that risk capital loss are imprudent or speculative.

The legal concept of how a prudent person should manage other people's money evolved from an early 19th-century precedent. One did not speculate with capital—a precept that kept common stock off the lists developed by states of legally acceptable investments for trustees and fiduciaries. The development of the Prudent Man rule stressed fixed-income obligations: they could be bought by a prudent person seeking income and preservation of capital.

It was only after the ravages of inflation that the public became aware that conservative prudence could also lead to capital loss. Ironically, the road to financial ruin could also be paved with good intentions. Perhaps speculating was not an unmitigated evil but a recognition that "riskless" investments also had their downside in the erosion of purchasing power.

Was it possible to hedge against inflation and other economic uncertainties by using speculative tools? While it sounded like a contradiction in terms, could speculating be used not as an end in itself but as a counterweight to a long position that was inherent in buying any security?

The answer, as it has evolved in the last decade or so, is a resounding yes. A whole string of derivative instru-

ments have been developed that both enhance pure speculation and act as a hedge against financial exposure. Thus
speculating is now a two-edged sword. It must be judged
not solely on its characteristics but on how it is used when
it is applied. The success of speculating also depends on
who is speculating and how perceptive the participant is.

Perhaps the worst mistake you can make in managing
your own money is to misunderstand or miscalculate the
limits of risk. You should be quite clear about the possibility of loss and the volatility of price.

Another common mistake is mismatching the investment or speculation with its intended purpose. If you have
treated a long-term conservative investment as a short-term
speculation, the reward is not likely to match the risk. For
example, borrowing substantial funds to buy raw land
based on the rumor of a shopping mall development may
commit you to supporting a negative cash flow (caused by
the large interest charges to carry the purchase) for far
longer than you anticipated.

And you can just as easily be at cross purposes with a
speculation. A short-term speculation becomes a long-term
investment when you aren't looking. For example, you
expect the price of gold to fall when the Group of Seven
finance ministers meets, so you sell gold shares short.
However, the meeting ends in disarray and the price of gold
appreciates. Instead of taking your loss, you maintain a
losing position.

It is important to understand your purpose in allocating
your funds. Only then can you rationally select the vehicles
or instruments to serve your intentions.

The purpose of speculating is naturally to make money,
but there are conditions that may deter you:

- Speculators need sufficient funds to participate, funds
  which may well be decimated in the course of speculating.

- Speculators need a high tolerance for price swings and volatility, both key elements in speculating.
- Speculators need to feel emotionally and/or psychologically comfortable with uncertainty.
- Speculators need to pay constant attention to their activities. No buy-them-and-put-them-away attitude will succeed.

If you feel comfortable with these conditions, speculating may be a game worth playing and worth winning.

A NOTE ON THE ORGANIZATION OF
THIS BOOK

The chapters in this book discuss the most popular speculative instruments: options, futures, commodities, precious metals and foreign exchange. But first we start with stocks and bonds as these are the most common instruments to be used in speculative fashion.

Since this book is the last in the series *Making the Most of Your Money,* it is based on the more detailed information provided in the previous works. If you are not familiar with the workings of the securities markets, you are cautioned to review those books before speculating.

Speculating can be extremely dangerous to your wealth. While it is possible to make a lot of money, it is also possible to lose more than you anticipated. Speculating is a high-risk game, regardless of how well hedged your positions are. (Of course, if you are perfectly hedged, then it might be argued that you are not speculating—but that is another school of thought.) Therefore, it cannot be stressed too strongly that you should not only know your risk tolerances, but you should assign speculation a role in the overall context of financial planning as outlined in *The Basics of Investing*.

Each chapter in this book is an entity unto itself and encompasses the information needed to understand how to speculate with that particular financial instrument. For speculators who like the idea of speculating and taking on risk but who do not have the time, energy or patience to develop their own programs, we have included a "Shortcut" at the end of each chapter. The shortcut indicates a number of mutual funds or managed accounts that, for a management fee and/or sales charge, will execute a speculation or run a whole portfolio of derivative instruments. They are presented only in alphabetical order, without any implied endorsement.

• 1 •

The Stock Market

ON THE MARGIN

Speculators in common stock wish to put more risk in their portfolios to obtain greater rewards. The traditional way to accomplish this is to use credit to buy more common stock than one's funds allow if the purchase is for all cash. Individuals can trade on credit, if they so desire, by establishing a margin account with a brokerage house. All brokerage firms offer margin accounts, but the conditions of credit vary from firm to firm.

Since using borrowed funds to invest is considered speculative by many investors, a preponderance of investors do not use credit or have margin accounts. However, margin buying and selling is an old, established practice. Whether it caused the Crash of 1929 (when speculators could buy stocks by putting up 10 cents on the dollar), as suggested by some historians, is a moot point. Margin accounts may also have contributed to some of the selling in the October 1987 meltdown as margin calls were anticipated, but they were hardly responsible for that precipitous market decline.

Margin buying is not a form of installment sales: the borrowed funds do not have to be paid back on any periodic schedule. When a transaction is completed sometime later by selling what was bought (at the option of the speculator), the borrowed funds are returned or credited to the broker.

To speculate with borrowed funds, you must open a margin account either with cash or securities that are subject to collateral. (Not all securities may be used for collateral. Check with the brokerage firm to see which are acceptable.) Most investment firms require a minimum of $2,000 to $3,000 in cash or $4,000 to $6,000 in marginable securities.

Many individuals who open margin accounts have two accounts—a regular account and a margin account—so there is no connection between the two. This is a sound practice since it separates investment and speculative activities; the latter cannot infect the former. It protects you from betting the ranch when you are feeling not only optimistic but lucky.

In a cash account, the investor buys and sells for cash, paying and receiving the full amount in the normal five business days required for routine settlements. Securities in a cash account may be delivered to the customer, or they may be kept in the brokerage house and credited to the investor's account in book-entry fashion.

In a margin account, the customer is borrowing the broker's funds. In turn, the securities are kept on deposit as collateral; they are kept in street name. This enables the brokerage firm to sell the securities if a margin call (an immediate demand for additional funds) goes unanswered, thereby protecting its funds.

Once a customer agrees to open a margin account, the brokerage firm will lend funds to buy stock or to buy additional stock, or it will simply supply funds as a loan against the collateral. How much will be lent is determined by two different sets of margin regulations: (1) the rules set by the Federal Reserve System (the Fed) and (2) the rules of the New York Stock Exchange.

Since the Fed is charged with controlling credit in the country, one of the valves it regulates is margin credit. Over the years the Fed has raised margin levels when there was too much credit in the economy causing inflationary pressures, and it has lowered margin levels when it wished to stimulate the economy.

Since 1974, the Fed has left the margin rate at 50 percent. This means that the customer must put up 50 percent, while the brokerage firm will lend the other 50 percent for the purchase of common stock. (The levels of margin are different for other kinds of financial instruments.) Thus, a $10,000 transaction requires the buyer and the broker to each deposit $5,000. They are, however, not partners in this endeavor: the customer bears all the risk.

Where the brokerage firm obtains the money to lend is of direct importance, since the rate it pays the bank is passed on to you, the ultimate borrower. The brokers' call money rate is published in the business section of the daily newspaper.

Depending on the size of your account and its activity, the brokerage firm will usually lend to clients at one or two percentage points above the call money rate. Margin borrowing is one of the cheapest ways to borrow funds for any purpose. You need not buy additional stock. The rate on the margin loan is constantly adjusted to reflect prevailing interest rates.

Since stock prices fluctuate daily, the New York Stock Exchange has established maintenance margin regulations to be sure that the borrowed funds are never in danger. This protection is for the lender rather than the borrower. Maintenance requires that the investor's ownership never be less than 25 percent (some firms use 30 percent) of the total market value of the purchased stock. If the market price has declined to that level, then a margin call will go out, requiring either additional cash or marginable securities.

For example, suppose you bought 200 shares of a $50 stock on margin: the $10,000 purchase was paid for by your $5,000 plus the broker's $5,000. Before you realize it, the share price falls to $35; your 200 shares now have a total market value of only $7,000. The $3,000 loss is solely yours. In other words, your equity is reduced to $2,000, and your account is now in imminent danger of a margin call. Some firms would have sent a call when the equity fell below 30 percent ($2,100), though others might have waited until it touched 25 percent ($1,750).

A *margin call* is a notification from the broker that a customer's account requires more funds or marginable stock. (All listed securities on the exchanges are considered marginable securities, plus many of the securities traded on the over-the-counter or OTC market.) If a customer does not comply, a portion of the account is sold to restore the maintenance level. Needless to say, an account that falls that far indicates not only a lack of attention but a violation of some commonsense precautions, such as a stop (loss) order.

There is one piece of street wisdom that says that you should never meet a margin call, based on the premise that you will be throwing good money after bad. Whether you do or not, remember that the stock in the previous example fell 30 percent; but to regain parity, it must rise by 50 percent—an uphill fight.

THE POWER OF LEVERAGE

Margin accounts give speculators credit, which in turn increases their leverage. The more credit, the greater the chance for enhanced profits. But bear in mind that credit also makes a margin account vulnerable. An account that uses a maximum of credit is rather like an inverted pyramid. Before examining the mechanics of margin trading, it is useful to see just how credit magnifies the rate of return on your funds. It is this amplification of the rate of return that makes credit so attractive.

When you deal with borrowed funds, it helps to understand the leverage factor: the greater the amount of borrowed money in an investment, the greater the leverage. Leverage can be expressed as a reciprocal of 1 minus the percentage of debt of the invested funds. If the debt is 75 percent of the investment, the leverage factor is as follows:

$$\frac{1}{1 - 0.75} = 4$$

In brief, the leverage factor is the number of times your funds go into the whole investment. At the current margin levels of 50 percent for common stock, the leverage factor is 2. For government bonds, the leverage factor is 20 since brokerage firms will lend (under current regulations) 95 percent of the necessary funds for purchasing Treasury paper.

This power of leverage is of course appealing to speculators because margin accounts make it possible to pyramid profits. To illustrate this buying power, assume once again that you deposit $5,000, borrow $5,000 through a margin account and buy 200 shares of the ABC Company at $50. The share price then rises to $75. You decide to sell: the profit of 25 points on 200 shares is $5,000. If you had not used credit, you would only be able to afford 100 shares in a cash account—a profit of $2,500, or 50 percent of the original equity. In the margin account you earned $5,000 on a $5,000 investment (before interest charges and commissions), or 100 percent. But there is no reason why you have to sell at $75. You have three options: (1) do nothing and let your profits run; (2) take your profits and sell; or (3) pyramid your profits by buying more on credit.

When prices go up, margin power is cumulative. As prices appreciate, the amount of purchasing power increases. Every extra dollar in a margin account's value releases two dollars for purchasing power. This can be used either to buy more of the same stock or to buy some other security, or it can be borrowed for another purpose.

Thus, you can exploit a trend. In the previous case, when the stock in the margin account reached $75, there was a profit of $5,000. With that sum, you can now buy 66 more shares ($5,000 ÷ $75). With another $25 increase, the original shares show an additional profit of $5,000, and the 66 shares earn $1,650, for a total of $6,650 of purchasing power. You might continue to pyramid and buy an additional 66 shares at $100. You now have 122 additional shares, plus the original 200, for a total of 322 shares worth $32,200. Remember, you started with $5,000.

To see what happens and to understand the profit potential of margin, it is necessary to appreciate how the margin account, or special miscellaneous account (SMA), operates. This is a temporary account that allows for the accumulation of equity in excess of what is currently required as prescribed by the regulations of the Federal Reserve System. For example, if you buy 500 shares of the XYZ Company at $20, the bookkeeping is as follows:

Market value	$10,000
Debit balance (borrowed from broker)	5,000
Equity (investor's funds)	5,000
50% of market value	5,000
SMA credit	0
Purchasing power	0

Prices then move up to $25:

Market value	$12,500
Debit balance	5,000
Equity	7,500
50% of market value	6,250
SMA credit	1,250
Purchasing power	2,500

With the additional purchasing power of $2,500, you buy 100 shares at $25 for a total of 600 shares:

Market value	$15,000
Debit balance	7,500
Equity	7,500
50% of market value	7,500
SMA credit	0
Purchasing power	0

At $30 you decide to take further advantage of margin borrowing by purchasing more shares with the $3,000 of purchasing power:

Market value	$18,000
Debit balance	7,500
Equity	10,500
50% of market value	9,000
SMA credit	1,500
Purchasing power	3,000

You now buy 100 more shares at $30:

Market value	$21,000
Debit balance	10,500
Equity	10,500
50% of market value	10,500

SMA credit	0
Purchasing power	0

When the price of the common stock moved from $20 to $30 (a 50 percent increase), your equity increased from $5,000 to $10,500, an increase of over 100 percent. Instead of controlling 250 shares in a cash account for the original $5,000, which at $30 are worth $7,500, there are 700 shares with a market value of $21,000.

Excess credit accumulates when prices advance. This excess purchasing power is periodically placed in the SMA. Of course prices retreat almost as often as they advance; and when you have two or three times more stock, the retreat can turn into a route. If the equity value of the account falls below 50 percent of the market value, it does not mean an immediate margin call.

In the previous case where the account had 700 shares, assume the price falls from $30 to $25:

Market value	$17,500
Debit balance	10,500
Equity	7,000

The equity is now less than 50 percent of the market value, $8,750. Since the account originally met the Federal Reserve requirements, no new deposits are necessary. Only when the account reaches a point where the equity is 25 percent ($4,375, or 30 percent for many firms—$5,250) does a margin call go out. If the debit balance exceeds the maximum loan value of the account's securities, the account is restricted. Sales in restricted accounts go to eliminating the restrictions (70 percent), and then the balance (30 percent) goes into the SMA.

Unless you are obliged to sell in the face of a margin call, it is up to you to terminate the position. Interest charges have a way of mounting up and should be monitored. After all, $5,000 at 12 percent amounts to almost $650 at compound interest in one year.

In the ordinary course of selling shares in a margin account, half of the proceeds are deposited to your SMA. In the previous example, 200 shares are sold at $30, reducing the market value by $6,000 but also the debit balance by an equal amount.

Market value	$15,000
Debit balance	4,500
Equity	10,500

The SMA receives a credit of $3,000, half the sale of the proceeds. If you decide to buy another security, you have $3,000 of purchasing power regardless of future market fluctuations.

A short sale can only be made in a margin account since you now owe stock that you had borrowed and sold in the anticipation of lower prices. You must deposit the same margin money, in addition to the proceeds of the sale. There are no interest charges for this arrangement.

A successful short sale also increases the value of the SMA. For example, you short 200 shares of the DEF Corporation at $20. You must deposit half of the market value—$2,000. The sale of the shares at $20 produces $4,000. Your account now has a credit balance of $6,000 and equity of $2,000. You have no credit in your SMA.

When the share prices descend to $15, as expected, the equity in the account rises by $1,000 to $3,000. You can evaluate the SMA by taking 50 percent of the market value of the shorted stock and compare it to the equity. There is an excess of $1,500 that is credited to the SMA.

Margin regulations and calculations are complex bookkeeping matters. Your broker can obtain the exact status of your account by consulting the back office for details.

Credit in a margin account provides leverage for the common stock speculator. Corporations also use credit in their business operations both for their short-term needs and their long-term capital requirements. The amount of debt a company uses is, of course, noted in the balance sheet. (The debt-to-equity ratio and other key credit ratios are discussed in *The Basics of Stocks,* Chapters 3 and 4.) Corporations that use a great deal of debt and that have debt-to-equity ratios greater than 25 percent are said to be leveraged. When the debt level exceeds 50 percent, they are said to be highly leveraged.

In general, the share prices of companies with a great deal of debt fluctuate far more than those of companies with little or no debt. Speculators are frequently drawn to such companies since price swings create profit opportunities.

CORPORATE LEVERAGE

If you are looking for a more speculative approach to common stocks (in addition to the use of margin), first analyze the financial components of a corporation. There is no ideal construct for a public corporation, and certain industries differ by a great deal. You cannot compare a steel company with a bank or a public utility with a high-technology business.

While there is no uniform model, there are some financial parameters that make some corporations more speculative investments than others. In recent years, the most critical element in determining risk is a company's creditworthiness. Nothing undermines investor confidence faster than a corporation's assumption of new debt, which weakens the stockholders' position.

At one time, debt was thought to be a sign of poor management; it was to be avoided. In the last generation, however, debt has been welcomed in many quarters. Treasurers and chief financial officers have aggressively borrowed to prove that they can achieve a higher return on borrowed funds than it cost to borrow those funds. Debt has become respectable, especially in the era of leveraged buyouts, takeovers, mergers and acquisitions—the restructuring of the American corporation. Not only has the ratio of debt versus equity grown, but the portion of earnings devoted to servicing that debt has jumped precipitously.

The companies that borrowed aggressively are now highly leveraged; that is, they are faced with huge fixed charges. Borrowing (whether it be short-term from a bank or long-term through the issuance of bonds) dramatically alters a compnay's earnings picture. If earnings are slim, the cost for servicing the debt can make a company look worse; if earnings are excellent, earnings can be magnified after servicing the debt.

To appreciate this phenomenon, consider the following three situations, which illustrate how "trading on the equity" exaggerates the results as it increases the risk:

1. Able Company has no debt. There are no fixed expenses to service debt. All earnings are shared by the stockholders.
2. Baker Company is financed by 50 percent debt and 50 percent equity. Fixed expenses are substantial.
3. Charlie Company's structure is highly leveraged with 90 percent debt and 10 percent equity. Debt services are extremely heavy.

Let's assume the same level of revenue for each company and the same number of shares outstanding. Notice in Table 1.1 how the earnings per share change after allowing for the servicing of the debt.

TABLE 1.1   Comparison of Earnings

	Able Co.	Baker Co.	Charlie Co.
Revenues	$20*	$20	$20
Fixed/variable costs	15	15	15
Net operating income	5	5	5
Debt	0	10	18
Interest charges	0	1	1.8
Earnings	5	4	3.2
Shares outstanding	1,000,000	1,000,000	1,000,000
Earnings per share	$5.00	$4.00	$3.20

*All figures are in millions of dollars except earnings per share.

The following year, revenues increase by 50 percent (see Table 1.2).

If revenues fall by 25 percent from the first year, earnings are devastated (see Table 1.3).

In summary, when earnings go up 225 percent for Able Company, the common stock is affected directly. In Baker Company, a rise of 256 percent in earnings translates into a similar increase in earnings per share. In Charlie Company, the result is remarkable as earnings per share increase almost 300 percent.

And, of course, it works in reverse. When earnings fall, the effect is out of proportion to the company with the greatest debt. In this case, though Charlie Company made money, earnings were wiped out by the debt service.

What does this leverage mean to the speculator? A great deal of debt on a company's balance sheet exaggerates the results. A major concern for the investment world is a company's ability to cover its fixed charges. A fall in revenues, and subsequently earnings, will naturally jeop-

TABLE 1.2   Comparison of Earnings—50 Percent Increase

	Able Co.	Baker Co.	Charlie Co.,
Revenues	$30*	$30	$30
Fixed/variable costs (+25%)	18.75	18.75	18.75
Net operating income	11.25	11.25	11.25
Debt	0	10	18
Interest charges	0	1	1.8
Earnings	11.25	10.25	9.45
Shares outstanding	1,000,000	1,000,000	1,000,000
Earnings per share	$11.25	$10.25	$9.45

*All figures are in millions of dollars, except earnings per share.

ardize that ability. If it becomes clear—either through weaker revenues, a restructuring of the corporation or the issuance of a new series of subordinate debentures—that a company is having problems, the price of its common stock will fall.

On the other hand, if revenues and earnings appear to be positive and outpace expectations, then it becomes equally clear that not only will earnings per share be better, but they will disproportionately exceed earlier estimates. Accordingly, the shares will move ahead sharply. It is this disproportionality that attracts speculators: they increase their risk factor through a company's skewed balance sheet. The greater the debt-to-equity ratio, the greater the chance for volatile market moves.

TABLE 1.3   Comparison of Earnings—25 Percent Decrease

	Able Co.	*Baker Co.*	*Charlie Co.*
Revenues	$15*	$15	$15
Fixed/variable costs (–10%)	13.5	13.5	13.5
Net operating income	1.5	1.5	1.5
Debt	0	10	18
Interest charges	0	1	1.8
Earnings (loss)	1.5	.500	(–300)
Shares outstanding	1,000,000	1,000,000	1,000,000
Earnings per share	1.50	.50	(–.30)

*All figures are in millions of dollars, except earnings per share.

A BETA BET?

To many investors, common stocks are, by definition, a speculation. It is true that stock prices fluctuate and are, by their nature, volatile. The price of a particular company's stock is tied to a large degree to the general moves of the market and, more specifically, to the earnings that a company generates. Whether prices move about randomly, as some observers suggest, or whether they trace trends that encourage predictions of future movements is, for the moment, beside the point.

What can be known with some certainty is the history of a company's volatility. Such volatility compared to the general market can be measured: it is the beta factor. *Beta* is the measurement of systematic risk, or risk that is common to all securities. (The beta number is derived from a complex formula, but the result is published by some financial services.) No amount of portfolio diversification will eliminate systemwide risk. A beta of 1 means that a particular stock has the same risk and volatility as the general market. A beta of less than 1 indicates less risk and volatility, and over 1 indicates more risk and volatility.

Anyone looking for additional excitement in selecting common stock can obtain it by choosing companies with beta rankings of 1 1/2 and 2 times the norm. This is not an invitation to a more speculative portfolio: it only means that the portfolio will have greater price swings. You will not lose or gain more capital with high beta stocks than with low beta stocks; you'll just do it faster.

Y•O•U•R M•O•V•E

- If you are willing to tolerate greater than normal risk in the stock market, consider opening a margin account. This account will enable you to borrow 50 percent of the transaction cost from the brokerage firm.
- Keep your regular investment activities separate from your margin purchases. In short, have two separate accounts—perhaps one with a regular full-service broker and the other with a discount broker to trade at cheaper rates.
- If you trade in a margin account, make sure you monitor your portfolio. Use market orders to protect your position.
- Margin loans are one of the cheapest forms of borrowing. Nevertheless, check the interest rate being charged your account to see that it is both competitive and not too onerous.
- The more speculative companies are potentially the most profitable ones to trade, but they are also the riskiest ones. Diversification is a sound market axiom, especially in new issues.

- Margin calls concentrate the mind. Before you answer one, make sure the reasons you bought the company remain unchanged.
- Highly leveraged companies usually exhibit greater price swings than those with little or no debt. Check on the debt-to-equity ratio before you buy a speculation.

S • H • O • R • T • C • U • T

Aggressive Growth Funds

- Acorn Fund
- Janus Fund
- Lehman Opportunity
- Over-the-Counter Securities
- Pennsylvania Mutual
- Phoenix Stock

• 2 •

The Bond Market

WHAT CAN BONDS RETURN?

"The rich are different," said F. Scott Fitzgerald. "Yes," Ernest Hemingway rejoined, "they have more money." Bonds are different from common stock—they have more credibility. Most people would rather be owed money than own equity. A bond is a fixed sum, and its conditions are virtually written in stone. Common stock, on the other hand, is subject to the vicissitudes of earnings, the conditions of the business cycle and changes in capitalization. As senior issues, bonds promise to repay what was lent plus interest. Common stock always has the potential of returning a far greater reward, and a far greater loss.

These characteristic differences mean that bonds never have the potential leverage associated with equity. Straight bonds offer little advantage to those interested in speculating on the fortunes of corporations in the marketplace.

So while bonds are less speculative than stocks, it does not mean that you cannot speculate in the bond world. Quite the contrary: bond speculation has more to do with the creditworthiness of bonds and interest rates than how well a corporation is doing and what its prospects are.

Most individual investors buy bonds for the long haul with little thought of selling them either before maturity or on some set future date. Price fluctuations are unimportant and for the most part, not even considered. Speculators, of course, are concerned with price, not yield to maturity. To buy bonds cheaply and sell them when they are dear, speculators must pay special attention to interest rates. It is the prevailing level of interest rates that dictates bond prices, as well as the direction and intensity of future inflationary (or deflationary) forces.

Furthermore, bond speculators must also consider the relatively large sums necessary to take a position in bonds where the standard bond is denominated in $1,000 units. To extend their grasp, they resort to a generous use of credit. Bonds are ideal to facilitate borrowing since they are backed not by an individual's promise to repay but by a large corporation or government agency.

Since the financial world considers debt a better form of security than ownership, bonds are more secure than stocks. Therefore, it is not surprising that brokerage firms and others will lend a relatively higher percentage of the market value of bonds than of stocks. For listed corporate bonds and some OTC nonconvertible bonds, the Federal Reserve System has set a 25 percent margin level. Thus, if you deposit $10,000 in a margin account, you can buy up to $40,000 of straight bonds.

Since there is an inverse relationship between the interest rate and the principal (when rates go up, principal goes down, and vice versa), speculators in bonds hope to be able to ride the interest rate wave. As interest rates surge upward, they want to be short bonds; when interest rates recede, they want to catch the upward surge of bonds by being long.

Therefore, the yield curve is an important indicator for bond speculators. It shows graphically the relationship of interest rates to fixed maturities. (For an analysis and the workings of the yield curve and interest rates, see Chapter 2 of *The Basics of Bonds.*) A normal yield curve, which is an upward-sloping curve, indicates that short-term money offers the lowest yields. As the time period is extended, yields rise. This is a reflection of the greater uncertainty of having the funds returned as well as the depreciation of their purchasing power because of future inflation. Long-term is clearly riskier than short-term, a notion borne out by the positively sloped curve. Speculators must make judgments on the direction of interest rates if they plan to trade bonds. Since interest-rate movements arrive with all the precision of spring rains, it is no easy call.

HOW DO YOU PREDICT INTEREST RATES?

No single item will provide the key to interest rates, whether it be a government statistic, a presidential proclamation, a meeting of central bankers or the pronouncement of some popular economist. A confluence of forces tends to push rates one way or the other. Professionals pay special attention to the following factors:

- Money supply
- Discount rate
- Gross national product
- Consumer price index
- Producer price index
- Commodity Research Bureau Index
- Price of gold
- Price of oil
- Trade deficits
- Federal deficits
- Employment/unemployment figures

And perhaps the most important factors are the comments and observations of the Federal Reserve System.

The financial world is somewhat fickle, giving preeminence to one factor at a time before it switches its affections to the next. It is important for investors as well as speculators to focus on interest rates since they help pinpoint the progress of the business cycle. You may not be able to call the exact turn in interest rates, but recognizing the trend makes it easier to be on the right side, whether it be for the long haul or a quick turn.

Speculating on reversals of interest rates provides the greatest fillip. If you can catch the major turns, such as the March–April 1987 reversal when rates headed sharply higher without much warning, you can profit handsomely thereby. In March 1989 the market witnessed another reversal as interest rates fell through July before firming. The Federal Reserve started to ease the federal funds rate and ease reserve conditions, fearing that its previous tight money policy was pushing the economy into a recession. Again, in 1991 the Fed continued to lower the discount rate and the federal funds rate to fight the recession and stimulate the economy.

WHICH BONDS ARE
BEST FOR SPECULATING?

Straight corporate bonds tend to move in concert when there is a change in interest rates. But all bonds do not move equally. There is some correlation, however, between quality of the issue and price change, and again between size of the issue and price:

- *Quality.* Bond prices are determined by many factors, but one of the most important is quality. In general, the highest-quality bonds (AAA) tend to sell at the highest prices or conversely at the lowest yields. The best-grade bonds are also the most stable and fluctuate in price less than inferior grades. Thus, if price fluctuation is the objective, a speculator should be examining not the top tier but lesser-quality bonds.

- *Quantity.* A shortage of supply or an abundance of demand affects the bond market, causing large spreads between the prices bid and asked. While it is possible for speculators to take advantage of this relationship, it is harder to buy or sell in quantity. Illiquid markets do not favor speculation.

You must recognize that pure speculating in the bond market is something of a contradiction in terms. The underlying motive in fixed-income investing is to search for and acquire the most solid, stable and creditworthy instruments. The bond market is truly risk-averse. Therefore, the speculator must turn the process on its head in looking for the issues that are the least stable, namely, those that will fluctuate most to provide trading opportunities.

This, of course, creates other problems. It is clearly dangerous to look for the worst investment, the "junk" of the bond world. *Junk bonds* (high-yielding instruments) are, for the most part, straight bonds with coupon rates that are 3, 5 or 7 percent greater than investment-grade issues. These bonds are bought largely by institutional investors for their high yields, not as speculations. Occasional turmoil in the junk bond market has shown that there is not much liquidity in this arena. Successful speculation calls for deep and continuous markets so that positions can be unwound when necessary.

It may be difficult for an individual speculator to buy (and/or short) junk bonds since it is a thin, largely institutional market. An individual might have a better chance to speculate in deep discount bonds. There are two types of deep discount bonds: (1) bonds that are issued at a deep discount usually with low coupon rates and (2) bonds that were initially issued at par ($1,000), but for various reasons have fallen on hard times.

Bonds initially bought at par have ceased to pay interest and are traded flat, that is, without accrued interest. These bonds are volatile for a few reasons. First, there is always the hope that conditions may get better since they are trading at levels that suggest that they cannot get much worse. Second, rumors, insinuations and even actual events, such as the reinstituting of interest payments, may propel such derelict bonds higher.

Volatility is also apparent in bonds that are still paying interest but have fallen dramatically in price because they have long maturities and coupon rates that are much lower than current interest rates. The lower the coupon rate, the greater the percentage change in the price of the instrument when interest rates rise or fall. Speculators looking at deep discount bonds should pay more attention to lower coupon bonds, even though roughly comparable bonds will have the same yield to maturity regardless of the coupon.

Perhaps the most volatile corporate bonds, those most sensitive to interest rate moves, are zero coupon bonds. Since they do not have any yield, they tend to fluctuate more than bonds with a fixed rate of return. Most zero coupon bonds are in the government market, but there are some corporate zero issues as well.

Another consideration for speculators is the cost of the carry—namely the out-of-pocket interest expenses while you use other people's money. High interest charges make speculating even more difficult. However, if you examine the cost to carry bonds, you will find that it is relatively inexpensive and, indeed, almost cost-free. Since an investment-quality bond may well have a coupon rate of 10 percent, it is not unlikely that a 12 percent or 13 percent margin loan makes the loan virtually free of charge.

For example, 40 $1,000 bonds with a 10 percent interest rate accounts for $4,000 of annual interest payments. To carry the 30 bonds on margin (since you only need to put up 25 percent margin for corporate bonds), the broker will charge interest to borrow, depending on prevailing rates and the size of the account. (Moreover, interest charges may well be a tax-deductible item, further sweetening the situation.)

The purpose is not to carry a bond portfolio cost-free but to make money on the swing in bond prices. Margin has enabled you to carry 40 bonds instead of 10. This additional leverage is only useful if bond prices do indeed move. While this is a conservative way of speculating in bonds, most aggressive speculators have now moved into the fixed-interest futures markets—whether they be bond contracts or options on the futures. (These will be examined in Chapter 3 under "Financial Futures.")

CONSERVATIVE BOND SPECULATING: CONVERTIBLE BONDS

If you wish to participate in prudent speculation, convertible bonds are made to order: they limit risk; they return more than common stock dividends, though somewhat less than the yield of straight bonds; they can be bought on credit in a margin account; and they provide a play on the common stock if a company is subsequently more successful.

The convertible bondholder is both speculating in bonds and holding an option to speculate and/or invest in common stock. All convertibles have an inherent investment value, that is, the price of the bond when stripped of its conversion features. What would it sell for as a straight bond? In other words, what credit criteria does it meet? What is its coupon rate? Its yield to maturity? What rating has been assigned by Standard & Poor's and other rating services?

Convertible bonds allow for conservative or prudent bond speculating. This hybrid instrument provides fixed interest income on one side, while it can partake of the rewards of equity if a company is successful. On the downside, the coupon rate keeps the convertible from sinking below comparable interest rate levels, acting as a floor. On the upside, the convertibles can be exchanged for a fixed number of common shares, assuming that the common stock has risen sufficiently to make the exchange profitable. (The conversion is, of course, optional unless there is a call provision.) For a fuller discussion of convertible bonds, see Chapter 8 of *The Basics of Bonds*.

In addition to the investment value, the speculator must assess the value of the conversion privilege. What are the present and future expectations of the common stock of the corporation? To evaluate the convertible, you must appreciate a number of relationships. The *conversion price* is the dollar amount of the bond equivalent to one share of common stock. If the conversion price is $25, then the conversion ratio (the number of times the conversion price goes into the par value of the bond) is 40.

The next factor to consider is the *conversion value*. This is the present market value of the number of shares into which a security can be exchanged. The conversion value is sometimes called the conversion parity. If the conversion ratio is 40 and the present market value of the stock is $30, then the conversion value is arrived at by multiplying the rate by the price—in this case, $1,200. This is the current theoretical value of the convertible bond; in reality, it may sell above (a conversion premium) or below (a conversion discount) the theoretical price. This can be expressed as a percentage. Thus, if the actual market price of the convertible is $1,200 with a conversion rate of 40 and the actual market price of the common stock is $27.50, the conversion value of the bond is $1,100. The conversion premium is 9.09 percent.

$$\frac{\$1,200 - \$1,100}{\$1,100} = 9.09\%$$

When a corporation issues convertible bonds, it sets the conversion point considerably above the level at which it was trading at the time the convertibles were issued. For the issuer, it is a way of raising capital now against what the stock price is projected to be in the future.

For the speculator interested in volatility, it is more profitable to buy the convertibles when the common stock is thoroughly depressed. At that point the convertibles will be selling at or around their investment value. There will be little or no conversion premium. (A speculator tries to avoid paying a conversion premium whenever possible.)

Only when the common stock appreciates will the bond start to trade at some premium above the investment value. There is no real leverage since the conversion value rises almost in lockstep with the value of the common stock.

As the price of the common stock rises further, the market price of the shares for which the bond can be exchanged will equal the bond's present investment value. The convertible will sell at a premium over conversion value since the interest yield is higher than the dividend yield.

Though the price of the common stock and the convertibles will rise proportionately once the price of the stock has passed the conversion threshold, the increased price in turn increases the market value of the bond because of the conversion feature.

If the convertible is purchased at a significant premium over the conversion value, it will probably see less than a proportionate increase in the value of the convertible when the common stock increases further in price. The reason for this is that the convertible buyer is essentially putting up more money for the equivalent shares than the price at which the shares are actually selling. The rule for the speculator is to avoid paying a conversion premium of any significance.

Speculators can enhance their leverage through the use of margin. Margin requirements for listed corporate convertible bonds are 50 percent, the same as for common stock.

The following are suggestions for successful convertible bond trading:

- Do not buy a convertible unless you think the company is going to be more successful than it is now.
- Buy convertibles only when the conversion premium is no more than 20 percent.
- Convertibles should return at least 3 percent more than the common stock if yield is a consideration. If not, the common stock might be a better buy.
- To lessen the chance of your convertible being called, do not buy any issue that sells for more than 20 percent of the call price.
- Buy the convertible when the common stock is in the doghouse. You are then obtaining the call on the stock for free. If the common stock fails to rise, the bond will eventually be redeemed at par.

SPECULATING IN JUNK BONDS

Speculative *junk bonds*—that is, bonds that are ranked below the top four investment grades of AAA, AA, A and BBB—are somewhat of a contradiction. Any bond yielding up to half a dozen percentage points above the prevailing rates for quality investments is rightfully suspect. The recent rage of junk issues in the 1980s has not been tested in a serious recession. However, the demise of Drexel Burnham Lambert in early 1990, perhaps the chief underwriter and market maker for high-yielding bonds, has certainly put a damper on this onetime exuberant market.

What makes junk bonds junky? Speculators buying junk bonds should appreciate the fact that these high-yielding bonds are a serious drain on a corporation's treasury. The coverage (the ratio of earnings dedicated to pay interest) on these service charges may be exceedingly thin.

If you are considering buying junk bonds, keep one simple ratio in mind: the coverage of senior charges (all interest expenses) can be determined by dividing the pretax earnings for capital by the senior charges. Whether the coverage is four or five times is perhaps less important than examining the trend over a series of years.

If coverage is skimpy and is becoming more so, bondholders will be skating on dangerous ice. If business activity turns down and earnings fall short, the likelihood for default increases. This is especially true of junk bond issues as they are usually subordinate to other debt issues.

If junk bonds are speculative, zero junk bonds are even more so. When a company issues zeros, it is admitting that its cash flow is so uncertain and tenuous that it is resorting to this device of putting off repayment until a later date or to maturity. The zero bondholder, in a worse-case scenario, will get nothing back in the event of default.

Nevertheless, junk bonds do provide both high yields and great volatility since the market is thin and erratic. A 15 percent return can double money in less than five years, but gains or losses of ten points ($100) in a day are not unheard of in the junk bond market.

It may be possible to buy high-yield bonds in a margin account, at the discretion of your brokerage house. This is a form of double leverage because of (1) the nature of the bonds and the indebted company's capitalization and (2) the borrowed money for the purchase. High yields more than offset borrowing costs, but it is nevertheless a tight-rope act recommended only to the very nimble.

How do you monitor the junk bond sector? One way is to measure the spread between seven-year Treasury bond yields and junk bonds. When the spread is great (anything over 4 percent), junk bond yields are high and the prices are low. A fear of credit deterioration in the economy, for example, can create this condition. When that fear subsides, the spread will narrow as junk bond yields fall; and conversely, the high-yield bond prices are likely to rally.

Junk bonds are certainly risky instruments with which to begin speculating. However, they are also volatile, making them an ideal vehicle for speculation. The one disadvantage is that the junk bond market is dominated by institutions; it is not easily accessible to individual speculators. To overcome that problem, a variety of junk bond mutual funds have sprung up to cater to speculators. They have the added benefit of spreading risk through diversification in their portfolios.

Y·O·U·R   M·O·V·E

- Speculating in the bond market can run the gamut from taking positions in conservative, investment-grade issues to buying junk bonds. The key to bond speculation is an accurate appreciation of interest-rate trends. You must study the yield curve to determine direction, plus the actions of the Federal Reserve System.
- Most corporate bonds can be bought in margin accounts. Whereas the margin level for common stock is 50 percent, corporate bonds can be bought for 25 percent. Before buying on margin, check your broker's loan rate to see that it is competitive. It should be one

or two percentage points over the broker's call loan rate published in the daily paper.

- Try to catch the major turns in interest rates because yield movement affects the whole market. In the stock market, some issues will always go up and others will always go down, regardless of whether there is a bull or bear trend. In the bond market, virtually all issues will move in concert—retreating when yields advance and advancing when yields retreat.
- Convertible bonds are a relatively conservative way to speculate. When you buy these hybrid securities, you have some downside protection because of the coupon rate. If the underlying common stock does well, you will have a respectable yield while waiting to convert.
- Junk bonds provide a speculator with the greatest price appreciation potential. They are also the riskiest bond speculation. If you are a plunger, select high-yielding obligations of substantial corporations. If your means are modest but your risk tolerance is great, consider a mutual fund.

S • H • O • R • T • C • U • T

These bond funds are not speculative per se, but they have had double-digit returns over the years. Other bond funds do use options and other trading techniques to raise their rates of return.

High-Grade Corporate Funds

- Calvert Income
- Mackenzie Fixed Income
- Vanguard Fixed Income Investment Grade

Convertible Bond Funds

- Dreyfus Convertible Securities
- SunAmerica Convertible Securities
- Zweig Convertible Securities

Junk Bond Funds

- Champion High Yield U.S.A.
- Merrill Lynch Corporate Bond High Income
- Value Line Aggressive Income

• 3 •

Commodity and Financial Futures

Producers, farmers and manufacturers have tradition-ally owned the product, crop or mineral that they are processing, growing or otherwise dealing with. Many months may lapse between the start and finish of their undertaking; the farmer's crop will not come in for many months and the miner or manufacturer may not be able to deliver for quite a while. All are faced with an exposure to risk: natural disasters and man-made catastrophes will af-fect the price of the product before they can sell or other-wise dispose of it. There is no certainty about what price they will obtain when they have the product ready for sale. The price might be lower than expected (producing a loss), or it might be higher than expected (providing a windfall).

Farmers, miners, oil drillers or other providers of com-modities are not interested in the chance of unexpected profits if it also entails the possibility of unexpected losses. They wish to fix their profits. To accomplish this they must find someone willing to buy the product or service—that is, take delivery in the future—at a predetermined price.

SPECULATORS VERSUS HEDGERS: A MATTER OF RISK

Futures contracts are financial devices for laying off risk. If a futures contract answers the concern of the producers who sell commodities, it also answers the needs of the processors, bakers, food distributors and others who need to be assured well in advance that they can buy these commodities at a predetermined price. Both sides are concerned with hedging their exposure to risk.

Futures contracts were devised to answer the common needs of sellers and buyers of commodities. Moreover, the commodity exchanges became the center for trading these contracts when it was clear that a futures contract did not have to be fulfilled by the original parties. A position in a contract can be terminated before taking or making delivery of the commodity by entering into an offsetting position.

The whole process is facilitated by middlemen, traders who are willing to enter into the process for only one reason—to profit. They accept the risk of price fluctuation because they hope to make money from their exposure. As a result, the business sector (the buyers and sellers who seek protection from uncertain prices or costs) is able to transfer its risk to the financial intermediaries.

In the futures markets, the buyers and sellers of commodities who try to protect themselves from price volatility are known as hedgers, and the financial intermediaries are the speculators. To better understand the relationship of hedgers and speculators, consider the cocoa market. No one knows more than Hershey, Nestle or Cadbury how treacherous the cocoa bean market can be. As hedgers, they act to protect themselves by nailing down market variables as much as possible.

Speculators have no interests to protect. If a chocolate bar manufacturer buys a six-month cocoa contract from a speculator for 10 metric tons at $1,850 per ton, the manufacturer is guaranteed delivery in six months of cocoa priced at $18,500. The speculator who sells the contract is now short one cocoa contract. (Since the clearing houses of the commodity exchanges guarantee the contract, neither party has to worry about the creditworthiness of the other. In practice, they don't know the identity of the other side of the contract.) If the price remains stable upon the delivery date (a most unusual situation), the parties are more or less even, except for commission fees.

The hedger takes delivery of the beans upon paying for the actual commodity; the speculator closes out his position by buying one contract. If the price had risen from $1,850 to $2,000 per ton, the hedger (the long position) would have a profit of $1,500 (10 tons × $150), and the speculator (the short position) would have a loss of an equal amount.

The long position could sell the contract for a profit or take delivery of the product, which would have been cheaper in comparison to the current cash price. (Cash and futures prices come together on the last day of contract trading.) The short position would grin and bear it.

If prices moved the other way and the price of cocoa had fallen to $1,700, the short position would have profited by $1,500 since the initial short sale was made at $1,850. The speculator would close out his position by buying the cheaper contract. The long position would either sell the contract for a loss or take delivery of expensive beans that currently could be bought more cheaply in the cash market.

THE MECHANICS OF THE
COMMODITY MARKET

Commodity trading is based on a few simple concepts that you should keep in mind if you intend to speculate:

- The commodity in question must be of standardized quality and must trade in standardized quantities. (You cannot have a diamond futures market since each gem is different and the diamonds are not interchangeable.)
- Buyers and sellers must have easy entry and exit to the commodity market. (Traders cannot be forced to queue up, nor can trading be done by appointment only.)
- There should be plenty of contending parties. (A few buyers or sellers tend to monopolize pricing.)
- A plentiful supply of market information is needed for the markets to reflect the best estimates of value.

Commodity markets share similar mechanical operations, whether trading foodstuffs or precious metals. Markets may have half a dozen (or more) contracts outstanding in the course of a year. You can buy or sell cocoa contracts for delivery in March, May, July, September, December or for the following March. For gold there are contracts for almost every month.

The size of a contract is specific to the market: in the cocoa market it is 10 metric tons; in silver, it is 1,000 ounces; and in pork bellies, it is 40,000 pounds. (See Table 3.1.)

Commodity contracts are bought with good-faith deposits. These "margin" deposits are different from the margin purchases of stocks and bonds. In those markets the securities must be paid for in full since ownership changes hands. You put up 50 percent of the value, and the brokerage firm lends you the other 50 percent at a given rate of interest. With commodity contracts, you only put up earnest money. No one puts up the balance and there are no interest charges since there is no change in ownership of the commodity, only the promise of a change.

The commodity broker (also known as a commission merchant) has to be reasonably certain that clients have sufficient net worth to cover a margin call if the market acts in a fashion contrary to what was anticipated. Many commodity brokerage firms will not open accounts unless clients can prove that they have sufficient capital to participate in this market.

Of course good faith only goes so far. Unlike the stock and bond markets, positions are marked to the market every day. This means that there is a daily tallying of gains and losses in your account. If the equity in your account falls below the minimum margin requirement, you will receive a margin call. This call requires you to deposit more funds immediately if the market goes against you.

Margin requirements vary from commodity to commodity, but to facilitate liquidity in the markets, they are kept relatively low—from 3 percent to 15 or 20 percent, depending on the volatility of the commodity.

This low margin requirement (plus the volatility) is enticing to speculators. The enormous leverage creates more risk, but a small change in a commodity's value creates a large change in the speculator's capital. For example, on a corn contract of 5,000 bushels valued at $12,500 (5,000 × $2.50 a bushel), a speculator might put up $500 (4 percent) as initial margin. If the price moved up by 10 cents (the limit for a daily move), the speculator would now have a contract worth $13,000. The value of the contract moved 4 percent ($12,500 × 4 percent = $500) to $13,000; however, the return on the invested capital was 100 percent. If the contract had retreated by a tic and was down 10 cents, all the original equity would be lost.

This skewed risk-reward relationship is the primary appeal of the futures market for speculators. It is possible

TABLE 3.1   Sample Commodity Markets and Futures Contract Information

& COMPANY

TOLL FREE NATIONWIDE   1-800-284-6000

Symbol for Exchanges

CBT	Chicago Board of Trade
CME	Chicago Mercantile Exchange
CMX	Commodity Exchange of New York
CSCE	Coffee, Cocoa, Sugar Exchange
IMM	International Monetary Market
KCBT	Kansas City Board of Trade
MACE	Mid American Commodity Exchange
MBT	Minneapolis Board of Trade
NYCE	New York Cotton Exchange
NYFE	New York Futures Exchange
NYME	New York Mercantile Exchange
WPG	Winnipeg Commodity Exchange

Symbol for Months

F–January	J–April	N–July	V–October
G–February	K–May	Q–August	X–November
H–March	M–June	U–September	Z–December

COMMODITY MARKETS AND FUTURES CONTRACT INFORMATION

COMMODITY	EXCHANGE	HOURS CST	MONTHS	Fluctuation Minimum	Value of a Tic	FUTURES Limit move	Contract Size	Minimum Tick	OPTIONS Limit Move	Strike Increments	MARGIN Initial	MARGIN Maint.	SPREAD Initial	SPREAD Maint
SOYBEANS	CBT	9:30-1:15	FHKNQUX	1/4 of a cent	$12.50	30 cents = $1500.00	5,000 Bu.	1/8 = 6.25	30 cents	25 cents	$1677.00	$1250.00	600	400
CORN	CBT	9:30-1:15	HKNUZ	1/4 of a cent	$12.50	10 cents = $500.00	5,000 Bu.	1/8 = 6.25	10 cents	10 cents	$700.00	$500.00	500	350
WHEAT	CBT	9:30-1:15	HKNUZ	1/4 of a cent	$12.50	20 cents = $1000.00	5,000 Bu.	—	—	—	$700.00	$500.00	500	350
OATS	CBT	9:30-1:15	HKNUZ	1/4 of a cent	$12.50	10 cents = $500.00	5,000 Bu.	—	—	—	$810.00	$600.00	500	350
SOYBEAN OIL	CBT	9:30-1:15	FHKNQUV	1 Point	$6.00	100 points = $600.00	60,000 lbs.	—	—	—	$877.00	$650.00	500	350
SOYBEAN MEAL	CBT	9:30-1:15	FHKNQUVZ	.10 cents	$10.00	10.00 = $1000.00	100 tons	—	—	—	$1000.00	$800.00	500	350
WHEAT KANSAS CITY	KCB	9:30-1:15	HKNUZ	1/4 of a cent	$12.50	25 cents = $1250.00	5,000 Bu.	1/8 = 6.25	25 cents	10 units	$1000.00	$700.00		
WHEAT MINNEAPOLIS	MBT	9:30-1:15	HKNUZ	1/4 of a cent	$12.50	25 cents = $1250.00	5,000 Bu.	1/8 = 6.25	20 units	10 units	$1000.00	$700.00		
SOYBEANS	MACE	9:30-1:45	FHKNQUX	1/4 of a cent	$2.50	30 cents = $100.00	1,000 Bu.	—	—	—	$350.00	$225.00	300	200
CORN	MACE	9:30-1:45	HKNUZ	1/4 of a cent	$2.50	10 cents = $100.00	1,000 Bu.	—	—	—	$150.00	$150.00	150	150
WHEAT	MACE	9:30-1:45	HKNUZ	1/4 of a cent	$2.50	20 cents = $200.00	1,000 Bu.	—	—	—	$250.00	$200.00	150	150
OATS	MACE	9:30-1:45	HJKNUZ	1/4 of a cent	$2.50	10 cents = $100.00	1,000 Bu.	—	—	—	$150.00	$150.00	150	150
JAPANESE YEN (A)	IMM	7:20-2:00	HMUZ	1 point	$12.50	No Limit	¥ 12,500,000.00	1 pt = 12.50	None	.01 cents	$2025.00	$1500.00	500	300
DEUTSCHE MARK (A)	IMM	7:20-2:00	HMUZ	1 point	$12.50	No Limit	DM 125,000.00	1 pt = 12.50	None	.01 cents	$2053.00	$1750.00	500	300
SWISS FRANC (A)	IMM	7:20-2:00	HMUZ	1 point	$12.50	No Limit	SF 125,000.00	1 pt = 12.50	None	.01 cents	$2053.00	$1750.00	500	300
US DOLLAR INDEX	CTN	7:20-2:00	HMUZ	1 point	$5.00	No Limit	500 x Index	—	—	—	$1000.00	$750.00		
BRITISH POUND (A)	IMM	7:20-2:00	HMUZ	2 points	$12.50	No Limit	£ 62,500.00	2 pt = 12.50	None	250 pts.	$2430.00	$1800.00	500	375
CANADIAN DOLLAR (A)	IMM	7:20-2:00	HMUZ	1 point	$10.00	No Limit	$ 100,000.00	1 pt = 10.00	None	.01 cents	$700.00	$575.00	500	375
AUSSIE DOLLAR (A)	IMM	7:20-2:15	HMUZ	1 point	$10.00	No Limit	$ 100,000.00	—	—	—	$1350.00	$1000.00	500	375
JAPANESE YEN (A)	MACE	7:20-2:15	HMUZ	1 point	$6.25	No Limit	¥ 6,250,000.00	—	—	—	$1250.00	$1000.00		
DEUTSCHE MARK (A)	MACE	7:20-2:15	HMUZ	1 point	$6.25	No Limit	DM 62,500.00	—	—	—	$1250.00	$1000.00		
SWISS FRANC (A)	MACE	7:20-2:15	HMUZ	2 points	$2.50	No Limit	SF 62,500.00	—	—	—	$1250.00	$900.00		
BRITISH POUND (A)	MACE	7:20-2:15	HMUZ	1 point	$6.25	No Limit	£ 12,500.00	—	—	—	$1250.00	$1000.00		
CANADIAN DOLLAR (A)	MACE	7:20-2:15	HMUZ	1 point	$5.00	No Limit	$ 50,000.00	—	—	—	$350.00	$275.00		
COMEX SILVER	CME	7:25-1:25	FHKNUZ	1/10 cents	$5.00	No Limit	5,000 ozs.	.1/cent	50 cents	25 cents	$1700.00	$1275.00	500	300
COMEX GOLD	CME	7:20-1:30	ALL	.10 cents	$10.00	No Limit	100 ozs.	.10 cents	$25.00	$10.00 (D)	$1300.00	$1100.00	400	300
PLATINUM	NYME	7:20-1:30	FJNV	$25.00	$5.00	$25.00	50 ozs.	—	$25.00*	—	$1500.00	$1005.00	300	210
PALLADIUM	NYME	7:10-1:20	HMUZ	1 point	$5.00	600 points = $600.00	100 ozs.	—	—	—	$1600.00	$1120.00	200	100
SILVER, NEW	CBT	8:05-1:25	GJMQV	1/10 cent	$1.00	50 cents = $500.00	1,000 ozs.	.1/cent	50 cent	50 cent	$500.00	$300.00		

					Daily Limit	Contract Size							
SILVER	MACE	ALL	1/10 cent	$ 1.00	.50 cents = $ 500.00	1,000 ozs.	—	—	—	$ 750.00	$ 500.00	200	100
KILO GOLD	CBT	GJMQVZ	.10 cent	$3.215	$50.00 = $1607.50	32.15 ozs.	—	—	—	$ 500.00	$ 300.00	200	100
GOLD	MACE	ALL	.10 cents	$ 3.33	$50.00 = 1650.00	33.21 ozs.	—	—	—	$ 600.00	$ 400.00	200	100
COPPER	CME	FHKNUZ	5 Points	$12.50	No Limit	25,000 lbs.	.10 cents	$25.00*	$ 5.00	$1100.00	$ 800.00	1600	1200
PLATINUM	MACE	FJNV	.10 cents	$ 2.50	$25.00 = $ 625.00	25 ozs.	5 points	None	.02 cents	$ 750.00	$ 500.00	750	500
ALUMINUM	CMX	FHKNUZ	5 Points	$ 4.00	No Limit	40,000 lbs.	—	—	—	$1500.00	$1125.00	700	525
PORK BELLIES	CME	GHKNQ	2½ points	$10.00	200 points = $ 800.00	40,000 lbs.	2.5 pts.	None	2C (E)	$1400.00	$1125.00	750	550
HOGS	CME	GJMNQVZ	2½ points	$ 7.50	150 points = $ 45.00	40,000 lbs.	2.5 pts.	None	2C (E)	$ 600.00	$ 400.00	400	300
LIVE CATTLE	CME	GJMOVZ	2½ points	$10.00	150 points = $ 600.00	40,000 lbs.	2.5 pts.	None	2C (E)	$ 700.00	$ 400.00	500	300
FDR CATTLE	CME	FHJKQUVX	2½ points	$11.00	150 points = $ 660.00	44,000 lbs.	2.5 pts.	None	2C (E)	$ 700.00	$ 400.00	500	300
LIVE CATTLE	MACE	FGJMOVZ	2½ points	$ 5.00	150 points = $ 300.00	20,000 lbs.	—	—	—	$ 350.00	$ 150.00	400	300
HOGS	MACE	GJMNQVZ	2½ points	$ 3.75	150 points = $ 225.00	15,000 lbs.	—	—	—	$ 350.00	$ 200.00	300	200
T-BONDS	CBT	HMUZ	1/32 point	$31.25	96/32nds = $3000.00	$ 100,000.00	1/64 = 15.62	128/64	2 basic pts	$ 2700.00	$ 2000.00	500	480
T-BONDS (B)	MACE	HMUZ	1/32 point	$15.625	96/32nds = $1500.00	$ 50,000.00	—	—	—	$ 1250.00	$1000.00		
T-BONDS (NITES)	CBT	HMUZ	1/32 point	$31.25	96/32nds = $3000.00	$ 100,000.00	1 pt. = $25.00	None	25 pts.	$ 2700.00	$ 2000.00		
T-BILLS	IMM	HMUZ	1 point	$25.00	60 points = $1500.00	$ 1,000,000.00	—	—	—	$ 1000.00	$ 700.00	200	150
MUNI BOND (B)	CBT	HMUZ	1/32 point	$31.25	96/32nds = $3000.00	$ 100,000.00	1 pt. - $25.00	None	25 pts.	$ 1500.00	$1500.00		
EURO DOLLARS (B)	IMM	HMUZ	1 point	$25.00	100 points = $3000.00	$ 1,000,000.00	—	—	—	$ 810.00	$ 675.00	200	150
CERTS OF DEPOSIT	IMM	HMUZ	1 point	$25.00	80 points = $2500.00	$ 1,000,000.00	1/64 = 15.62	128/64	2 basic pts	$ 750.00	$ 500.00		
T-NOTE	CBT	HMUZ	1/32 point	$31.25	96/32nds = $2000.00	$ 100,000.00	—	—	—	$ 1350.00	$1200.00		
CRB INDEX	NYFE	KNUZ	0.5 points	$25.00	No Limit	500 x INDEX	—	—	$ 5.00	$ 1750.00	$ 1325.00	500	400
S&P 500	CME	HMUZ	5 points	$25.00	No Limit	500 x S&P INDEX	.05 = $25.00	—	—	$22000.00	$8000.00	500	300
KANSAS CITY VALUE LINE	KCBT	HMUZ	5 points	$25.00	No Limit	500 x VL INDEX	—	—	—	$10000.00	$7500.00	500	300
KC MINI VALUE LINE	KCBT	HMUZ	5 points	$ 5.00	No Limit	100 x VL INDEX	—	—	—	$ 2000.00	$1500.00		
NYFE INDEX	NYME	HMUZ	5 points	$25.00	No Limit	500 x NYFE	.05 = $25.00	None	$ 2.00	$ 9000.00	$6000.00	500	300
MMI MAXI	CBT	ALL	0.5 points	$12.50	No Limit	250 x MMI	—	—	—	$21000.00	$8000.00	1000	800
COFFEE	CSCE	HKNUZ	1 point	$ 3.75	600 points = $2250.00	37,500 lbs.	1 pt.	None	.05 cents	$ 2000.00	$1500.00	800	475
COCOA	CSCE	HKNUZ	1 point	$10.00	88 points = $ 880.00	10 MT tons	1 pt.	None	$100.00	$ 850.00	$ 650.00	500	300
COTTON	NYCE	HKNUZ	1 point	$ 5.00	200 points = $1000.00	50,000 lbs.	1 pt.	None	100	$ 2000.00	$1500.00	500	400
SUGAR	CSCE	HKNUZ	1 point	$11.20	50 points = $ 560.00	112,000 lbs.	1 pt. = 11.20	50 pts.	100 pts.	$ 1250.00	$ 910.00		300
ORANGE JUICE	NYCE	FHKNYX	5 points	$ 7.50	500 points = $ 750.00	15,000 lbs.	5 pts.	None	$250	$ 4000.00	$3000.00	500	300
LUMBER	CME	FHKNUX	10 cents	$15.00	500 points = $ 750.00	150,000 bd ft	.10 cents	None	$10.00	$ 1200.00	$ 800.00	550	450
CRUDE OIL	NYME	ALL	1 point	$10.00	100 points = $1000.00	1,000 barrels	1 pt.	None	100 pts.	$ 2000.00	$1500.00	500	300
GASOLINE	NYME	ALL	1 point	$ 4.20	200 points = $ 840.00	42,000 gals	1 pt.	None	—	$ 2000.00	$1500.00	500	300
HEATING OIL	NYME	ALL	1 point	$ 4.20	200 points = $ 840.00	42,000 gals	1 pt.	None	2C(E)	$ 2000.00	$1500.00	500	300
ALUMINUM	CME	FHKNUZ	5 points	$20.00	100 points = $2000.00	40,000 lbs.	1 pt	None	—	$ 2000.00	$1500.00		

(A) EFP MARKETS
(B) NIGHT BONDS

BP 22 RM-CAL (12/91)

*PLEASE NOTE that margins are subject to change without Notice. If you have any questions about margins, contact the margin department.
All statements made herein, while not guaranteed, are based on information considered reliable and are believed to be accurate.

SOURCE: Courtesy of Ira Epstein & Company. Call 1-800-284-6000.

to reap an enormous return in relatively short order. It is also highly risky since minor price fluctuations can quickly put an account in a deficit position.

If the market had gone against the speculator, the commodity house would then require additional margin, known as maintenance margin. This is required on a daily basis and funds must be wired, though some houses will accept personal checks. A maintenance margin deposit should bring an account back to the level of the initial margin.

FINANCIAL FUTURES

The most common way to speculate on bonds and other debt instruments is through the financial futures markets. (In Chapter 2 we discussed some of the techniques for speculating in bonds without using the commodity markets.) Financial futures are not only tools for speculators: they are useful for conservative investors interested in hedging their portfolios.

Financial futures operate the same way as commodity futures do but with one exception. The hedger in commodity contracts is worried about price fluctuation caused by unpredictable events. In grains, the hedger is worried about drought, floods or locusts; in metals, labor strikes by miners; and in oils, an explosion in a major field or a huge oil spill. But in financial futures, hedgers worry about the cost of money as represented by interest rates. How do you hedge against the rising or falling cost of money?

Financial in futures were only developed in the mid-1970s as fluctuations in interest rates started to accelerate. Inflation pervaded the fixed-income market, causing bonds to depreciate. The Chicago exchanges used commodity contracts as models for financial contracts to protect against interest rate risk.

That risk was all too real: the price of a 10 percent bond selling at par, 100 ($1,000), would fall to 90.9 if prevailing interest rates moved to 11 percent; conversely, the price would move to a premium of 111.1 if interest rates fell to 9 percent—depending on maturities. Institutional money managers, portfolio planners, banks, insurance companies and other long-term fixed-income investors needed a hedge against this volatility.

The first financial futures contract to be tried was based on U.S. Treasury bonds, and it was an immediate success. The T-bond was a natural since the government securities market is the most interest-sensitive market in the world. It instantaneously reflects all information that affects interest rates, whether it be congressional hearings, executive budget proposals, Federal Open Market Committee activity, prime rate moves of the commercial banks or international central bank intervention.

Moreover, the government debt market has extraordinary liquidity: billions of dollars are traded hourly. And trading does not take place in 1/8ths or 1/4ths but in 1/32nds and 1/64ths as a reflection of its fine-tuning. In short, no other financial market is as broad or as deep.

The key features of the T-bond contract as traded on the Chicago Board of Trade are as follows:

- Basic trading unit: U.S. Treasury bonds with $100,000 face value
- Deliverable grade: U.S. Treasury bonds, maturing at least 15 years from delivery day if not callable; and if callable, they cannot be called for at least 15 years from delivery day
- Price quotation: Expressed as a percentage of par (e.g., 92-01 means 92 1/32)
- Minimum fluctuation: 1/32 of a point ($31.25 per contract)

- Daily price fluctuation limit: 64/32 ($2,000 per contract) above and below the previous day's price
- Initial margin: $3,000 per contract
- Maintenance margin: $2,500
- Hours of trading: 8 A.M. to 2 P.M. (Chicago time)

The financial press provides a daily table for T-bonds that shows a dozen or so contracts, maturing every three months and extending out for almost two years (see Table 3.2).

The September bond contract in Table 3.2 opened at 93-02, which is a percentage of par: $930.625 per $1,000, or $93,063 for a $100,000 contract. It settled down 1/32 on the day, or $31.25 per contract. The settlement price of 93-01 translates into a yield of 8.744. (Treasury bond yields are based on a hypothetical 8 percent, 20-year coupon bond. Deviations from the standard are allowed in execution but must be adjusted to conform to the standard.)

Given the example in Table 3.2, a speculator could sell short a T-bond futures contract at 93-01. In other words, the speculator would promise to deliver a $100,000 (face value) U.S. Treasury bond meeting all the noted specifications: at the time, however, it is only a promise since the speculator doesn't own any bonds and thus is short the instrument. To take that position, the speculator must do two things:

1. He or she must make a margin deposit of $3,000 (some brokerage houses may require more) as earnest money,

TABLE 3.2 Sample Daily Table of T-Bonds

Sept.	Open	High	Low	Settle	Change	Yield Settle	Change	Open Interest
	93-02	93-05	92-23	93-01	−1	8.7444	+.004	135,000

not the $93,031.25 that the T-bond is currently trading at, or the $100,000 face value.

2. He or she must expect interest rates to rise (which in turn will cause the price of bonds to fall). The speculator's profit is directly proportional to how far the bond's price falls.

Of course, the speculator may guess wrong: interest rates could head south and bond prices north. The seller's loss, then, is directly proportional to the bond's gain.

Double or Nothing?

Assume that the speculator has made a correct prediction of interest rate movements: they go up and before the expiration date of the contract, the September bond has moved to 90-30 ($90,937.50), for a drop of 2-03, or $2,093.75. The speculator now has two ways to pocket the profit. Since the speculator holds a short position, purchasing an equivalent bond will end the obligation to deliver. That is the customary way of terminating a short position. A speculator must make an offsetting position to close out a position—buy a contract if short, sell a contract if long.

However, a few speculators will opt for the second way—to deliver the actual bond that they purchase in the open market (at a price clearly below the one where the speculator went short) to the clearinghouse corporation of the exchange. This is a more awkward way to end a futures position, not to mention a more expensive way, but the system will accept any deliverable bonds, adjusting for coupon rates and maturity.

The speculator has made $2,093.75 on an initial margin deposit of $3,000, a 43 percent gain. Had interest rates gone lower, the speculator would have lost as bonds rose in value. At a price of 95-01, he or she would have lost $2,000.

But a margin call would have gone out before the loss had reached that point.

A naked short sale is dangerous, especially without stop orders to limit loss, or simply inattention. Speculation requires constant diligence since even the government bond market can move dramatically on some untoward piece of news.

It is important to understand what the hedger is trying to accomplish on the other side of the trade. Assume that an investor in July is holding $500,000 of U.S. Treasury bonds, 12 3/4 of 2005 in a portfolio, with a long position fully paid for. At the end of the year, the bonds will have to be sold since the funds are needed elsewhere. The investor can wait the six months before the sale, drifting on the tide of interest rates, which may make the bonds either more valuable if rates go down or less valuable if rates go up.

Another choice is available: hedge against interest rate fluctuations by going short in the futures market. The bonds are presently priced at 113.25, yielding 8.81 percent. By selling ten December contracts at 92-16, the investor hopes to hedge against an interest rate increase that will lower the value of the bonds. Assume that interest rates do rise, and the bonds consequently fall. However, the futures contracts have also fallen, offsetting the loss of the long bonds. Table 3.3 shows this classic short hedge.

The loss of $26,250 in Table 3.3 is far better than the $101,250 loss that would have been suffered had the position not been hedged. (The reason that the hedge is not balanced on a one-to-one basis is that the dollar value of higher coupon bonds changes by a larger dollar amount than the dollar value of lower coupon bonds. Remember that the bond contract is based on an 8 percent coupon; therefore, it is necessary to use a greater number of contracts for optimal coverage.)

TABLE 3.3   A Classic Short Hedge

Cash Market	Futures Market
July	*July*
Holds $500,000 12 3/4 T-bonds due 2005 Market price: 113.25	Sells 10 T-bond futures contracts at 92-16
December	*December*
Sells $500,000 12 3/4 T-bonds at 93.00	Buys 10 T-bond futures contracts at 85-00
Loss: $566,250	Gain: $925,000
$\underline{465,000}$	$\underline{850,000}$
–$101,250	$ ·75,000
Balance: –$101,250	
$\underline{75,000}$	
–$ 26,250	

Whether long bonds were held fully paid or in a margin account, the results would have been similar. A speculator could establish a long position of $500,000 T-bonds on margin for about $25,000 in a margin account, assuming that interest rates were going down. But an exposed position is uncomfortable, so a short position is also established just in case the interest rate assumption was wrong. The short position can fully hedge or partially hedge the long position, depending on how much protection the speculator feels comfortable with. Since the short position is a hedge, the hedging margin is less, as little as $1,500 per futures contract.

Hedging reduces both the exposure and the potential for speculative profit. For the investor with the long position, the portfolio is safeguarded against interest rate risk and possible loss by using futures. For the speculator, the hedge is a way of protecting against extreme loss, but it also denies the realization of full speculative profit.

TREASURY BILLS: A SMALLER SPECULATION

T-bonds are the most popular of the financial futures, but there are other interest rate instruments that may be used for hedging or speculative activity. T-bills and Eurodollars are two contracts that match T-bonds in that the basic trading units are $1 million. However, there are contracts for T-notes, T-bills and Ginnie Maes where trading units are $100,000. The various exchanges have different sizes and expiration dates for their own contracts.

While the principles and mechanics of trading these interest rate contracts are similar, there is some difference in volatility. Near-term instruments (such as T-bills and Eurodollars) tend to react most quickly to interest rate changes. Some speculators plot the differences between the least volatile (such as T-bonds) and the most volatile (such as Eurodollars). The differential is thought to be a leading indicator for a change in the direction of interest rates.

Since hedgers are usually long in the actual instruments (that is, they have a position in T-bonds, Eurodollars or some other interest-sensitive obligations), the speculators are long in the futures contracts since the hedgers are the ones who sold the futures short. That short hedge is most common, but a long hedge is also possible.

If the hedger is expecting funds to lend or invest for a short period (say, three or six months), when they are received in a few months time, it is possible to take a position against falling interest rates by buying futures contracts. The purchase of futures contracts means that the hedger will receive at the expiration a three-month or six-month T-bill. The seller of the contract (in this case, the speculator) is obliged to furnish the T-bill. While the hedger is expecting lower rates (and a higher bill), this step will lock in the higher rates (and a lower bill). The contract has appreciated, which offsets the higher actual price when the funds are received. The speculator, who is short the contract, is hoping for higher rates (and a lower bill). If the rates do go up, the contract will depreciate in value, as will the actual bills; if the rates go down, the speculator will be able to cover with cheaper bills.

Or the money manager can hedge against rising short-term interest rates in the immediate future by selling a T-bill contract for future delivery. If rates rise after the sale but before the delivery date, the value of the contract will depreciate. However, the hedger can profit by buying back at a lower price the contract that was sold at a higher price. The speculator would have bought the futures contract with the hope that before the expiration date, the rates would fall and the value of the contract would appreciate.

Whatever the combination, the hedger in interest rate futures (as well as other commodity contracts) tries to protect a current long position or a future short position by using futures contracts that result in an equal and opposite effect. The hedger, regardless of whether it is a short or long hedge (or some combination of spreads—the establishing of positions in opposite directions in the same item), protects from loss by foregoing gain. The speculator, on the other hand, does not have to work both sides of the street since there is no position to protect. Speculators must concentrate solely on determining the direction of interest rates. The assumption of risk, which is literally open-ended in the futures markets, is worthwhile only if there is the potential for great gain.

To help appreciate the cause and effect of interest rate movements, Figure 3.1 lists a number of significant economic situations. Futures contracts react to credit conditions. If you can understand those credit conditions, you can anticipate the price direction of the futures market.

Markets have their own internal logic. While the actions in Figure 3.1 may prompt financial futures to follow a given direction, markets seldom act in isolation or on only

FIGURE 3.1   Interest Rate Movements' Effect on Futures

Action	Reason	Direction
Federal discount rate increases	Less bank credit reduces funds availability	⇓
Federal discount rate decreases	More bank credit expands funds availability	⇑
Money supply increases	Easier money, inflation fears cause Fed funds to rise	⇓
Money supply decreases	Tighter money cools inflation and lowers Fed funds	⇑
Fed repurchases or buys bills	Adds reserves to banking system, interest rates fall	⇑
Matched sales or sells bills	Drains moneys from banking system, rates rise	⇓
CPI rises	Inflation heating up	⇓
Disposable income rises	More consumption, inflation possible	⇓
GNP falls	Slower economic growth	⇑
Housing starts rise	Fed may tighten credit to slow expansion	⇓
Inventories up	Weak sales, economy soft	⇑
Leading economic indicators up	Anticipates stronger economy, credit demand	⇓
Petroleum prices fall	Cools inflation, lowers interest rates	⇑
Precious metals prices fall	Fear of inflation abates	⇑
Producer price index (PPI) rises	Potential inflation, investors demand higher interest rates	⇓
Unemployment rises	Economy slowing, easier credit	⇑

one impetus. At any time, a number of forces are present: the results may not only be enigmatic, but they may even be contrary to what was anticipated. Only by constantly observing what is actually happening can you develop a sense of market trends.

Y · O · U · R   M · O· V· E

- Commodity trading is a fast-paced game. You must be ready to commit a great deal of attention if you want to participate. Unless you can monitor your positions several times a day, you may not only miss opportunities but risk substantial losses.

- Make sure you have adequate capital reserves to protect your trading account. A shortage of funds will force you out of positions when they temporarily move against you.

- Remember that the small down payment for a commodity contract is just earnest money. The enormous leverage in commodity and financial futures exposes the speculator to great losses—perhaps all of his or her capital.

- Successful traders concentrate on a few select commodities to understand the nature of a specific market. They also develop and closely follow patterns, whether they be the cyclicality of product demand or technical indicators.

- Financial futures appeal to speculators who are skilled at predicting interest rate trends. Investors may safeguard their long positions in debt instruments by hedging through the sale of financial futures. This offsets the exposure incurred by holding fixed-income investments.

- If you do not have the time or the temperament for the futures markets but nevertheless wish to participate, consider hiring a commodity trading adviser. You may also hire a firm to evaluate a number of commodity trading advisers, but they usually require the speculator to have $100,000 of risk capital to invest.

S·H·O·R·T·C·U·T

Commodity and Financial Futures Advisers

- Dunn Capital Management
- Futures Management
- George Booth & Associates
- Jones Commodities
- Orion

Consultants To Evaluate Commodity Trading Advisers

- Barclay Trading Group
- Managed Account Reports
- Princeton Futures
- Strategic Commodity Systems

• 4 •

Options

Options are speculative tools that enhance the potential for profit through leverage. By putting up a small amount of money, you control shares worth far more for a short period. An option is a contract that may be used by either an investor or a speculator, depending on which side of the contract one undertakes. There are two kinds of options: (1) a call option and (2) a put option.

A call option is a right (but not an obligation) to buy 100 shares of stock at a fixed price before a set expiration time. This call option can be bought for a premium, a price that is a fraction of the face value of the underlying shares.

A *put option* is a right (again, not an obligation) obtained by the buyer for the price of the premium to sell 100 shares of stock at a set price before a fixed expiration period. If the buyers of puts and calls do not exercise their options, they will then expire worthless. However, sellers of puts and calls are under an obligation to put or fulfill their side of the bargain—to take stock in case of a put or sell stock in case of a call at those predetermined prices. The exchanges have clearing corporations that oversee compliance by both parties.

Options can serve many different purposes:

- They are a cheap way of participating in the stock market for a limited time.
- They can diversify a portfolio.
- They can spread and limit risk.
- They can provide additional income for investors.
- They can provide leverage for speculation.

Like commodity futures contracts, options have been part of the financial world for a long time. However, it is only recently that options have been publicly listed on the exchanges to facilitate trading. Before the 1970s, stock options were used, but they were a private arrangement between the seller and the buyer of the option. In 1973 the Chicago Board of Trade created the Chicago Board Options Exchange, which was an immediate success for all parties involved in option trading.

Before the stock market crashed in October 1987, the options markets were dominated by small investors. The appeal was simple: while you might buy a round lot (100 shares) of IBM at $110 per share for a total of $11,000, you could buy a 90-day, at-the-money call (where the strike price of the option equals the market price of the underlying stock) for about $7.00 (or $700 for a 100-share contract). With the purchase of the call, you could control 100 shares of IBM for 90 days (the duration of the contract).

If the price advanced past $117 ($110 for the stock plus $7 for the option) before the expiration date, you would be on the verge of profiting from the appreciation of the stock. You would then have the choice of either selling the option contract (which also appreciated in a commensurate way) or actually calling the shares by paying the seller of the option $110 per share.

In a bull market such as the one preceding the crash, the options exchanges offered the small investor an inexpensive ticket for boarding the express train. Many small investors did not buy calls or puts but decided to sell them.

This turned into a problem for a number of investors, for they did not understand the characteristics of options. Options are generally proposed as being riskless, or in the words of advertising, "You can never lose more than you put up."

This, of course, is true if you buy a put or a call, but it is emphatically not true if you sell one. This is especially true if you are selling "naked" puts or calls—that is, selling what you do not own and may not be able to afford, or what you may not be able to accept and pay for when put to you. Selling calls and puts leaves the seller with an open-ended exposure—a fact all too frequently omitted by overly zealous brokers in suggesting ways to obtain higher yields.

When the market fell on Meltdown Monday, the price of the index fell dramatically, and conversely, the price of puts soared so that it was enormously expensive to close out positions. More than a few investors who had put up a few thousand dollars to earn some easy money found that they had lost literally hundreds of thousands of dollars through a speculation they did not understand. What they should have understood, without understanding the mechanics of options, is that there is no "easy" money in speculating or any other endeavor.

Since hundreds of million of dollars were lost in the crash in the options market, it should be clear what went wrong. Too many people were sold the idea that they could make a little extra easy money by selling naked puts.

Unlike some other speculative instruments, options provide leverage without the use of borrowed funds. In that sense, they can lower your risk without your incurring any interest charges. You can undertake a position in the market without using credit.

Option buyers need to put up only the price of the premium, which may range from 5 to 15 percent of the market value of the underlying shares. No credit is allowed for the purchase of options, and brokerage houses will not lend funds to buy options. Option sellers are required to deposit margin since there is a potential for losses. (The exact amount depends on what else is in the account, as well as the requirements of the brokerage firm.)

There are options on many financial instruments: options on bonds, options on futures contracts, options on foreign currencies and options on indexes. The following discussion will first deal with options on common stock, since these are the most popular options.

THE EASY OPTIONS: COMMON STOCK

All options have a common language, though the products, the exchanges and just about everything else will be different. The following terms—call options, put options, exercise or strike price, premium and expiration date— must be explained in detail.

Call Options.   A call option based on stocks gives the buyer a limited right (but never an obligation) to buy shares of a company at a set price within a set time period. For example, the buyer of a call option of the ABC Corporation on January 3 has the right to purchase stock at $50 a share to be exercised within 180 days. (In reality, options expire on the last day of the third week of the expiration month.)

The underlying securities are traded in a round lot of 100 shares. There are call options on over 200 listed corporations on the Chicago Board Options Exchange, the American Stock Exchange, the Philadelphia Stock Exchange, the Pacific Stock Exchange and the New York Stock Exchange.

Put Options.   A put option gives the buyer the limited right (but not an obligation) to sell the underlying securities of a public corporation listed on one of the major option exchanges. The price of the sale and the expiration of the option is fixed when the option is bought.

Exercise or Strike Price.   The exercise price, or strike price, is the price at which the buyer of the call has the right to buy the underlying shares. It does not change, regardless of any movement in the actual stock price. For the put buyer, the exercise price is the one at which the holder has the right to sell 100 shares of the underlying security.

There may be a number of options for each underlying security, each with a different strike price. Each exercise price will carry a different premium, depending on whether it is at the money, in the money or out of the money. For example, the actual price of the underlying shares may be $50, but there will be exercise prices above ($55, $60, $65) and below ($45, $40, $35). Each of those exercise prices will command a premium that is based on whether it is profitable or not and on the amount of time left until the expiration date.

Premium.   Each exercise price had a different premium, that is, the price paid to acquire the call or put option. Premiums are based on two factors: (1) the intrinsic value of the option, and (2) the time value of the option. If an option has a strike price of $55 (when the current price of the underlying shares is $50), then a premium of $6.50 reflects an intrinsic value of $5 plus a time value of $1.50.

Expiration Date.   The value of options diminishes with time. The clock is always against the option buyer as the possible exercise period inexorably runs out. When the expiration date is reached, the option has lost any value. Therefore, timing is critical since the option buyer is holding a wasting asset.

The intrinsic value of the option is calculated by one of three conditions of the option's price. As noted previously, the option can be at the money, in the money or out of the money. An option that is *at the money* is one in which the market price of the underlying security is the same as the strike price. *In the money* indicates that the market price of the stock is above the strike price, while *out of the money* shows the market value to be below the strike price.

An at-the-money call option has no intrinsic value; it only has time value. A call that is out of the money also has no intrinsic value but only has time value because there is no (profitable) difference between the lower market price and the higher strike price. However, a call option that is in the money has both intrinsic value (the difference between the higher market price and the lower strike price) plus time value.

Buyers of options hope to profit by a substantial and sustained move in the price of the underlying shares. This move will increase the value of all the options, whether at the money, in the money or out of the money. However, an option only becomes profitable when it either exceeds its purchase price so that it may be sold or increases sufficiently so that it may be exercised for the underlying shares. To be profitable, the price of the underlying shares has to rise sufficiently to cover the cost of the premium.

AND FOR THE SELLER . . .

Speculators should consider the profitability of selling options. Many speculators are prone to buying options on the basis of an intriguing story, a major development about to come to fruition, a technical breakout on a chart or a simple hunch. If the news is positive, calls are bought; if negative, puts are bought. Either activity protects no position since the speculators do not own the underlying shares.

On the other hand, conservative investors are likely to sell calls on the shares they own and puts on their short sales. They wish to protect an already established position and at the same time earn some additional income. If they can improve the rate of return of their portfolios through the sale of options, so much the better. Some speculators also sell options without a position to protect: they are trading naked. As we saw in the October crash, this is a dangerous practice and not one for novices.

Option sellers receive the premiums (less commissions) that the option buyers pay. For that income, the sellers are obliged to perform according to the terms of the option. If the buyer of a call option exercises the option, the seller must deliver the shares at the agreed price, regardless of the current market price of the shares. In the case of a put option, the writer must purchase the required number of shares at the strike price, regardless of the market price.

The premium is determined by the forces noted previously—that is, time value, intrinsic value, supply and demand, interest rates and volatility. The premium income is important to sellers, and it affects their projected rate of return. If a call is written on the ABC Corporation at $6.50, the seller gains $650 ($6.50 per share × 100 shares). If that is done twice in the course of a year, the seller takes in an additional $1,300 plus the normal dividends, if any.

On a $50 stock, the option seller has added $1,300 (26 percent per annum) if the shares do nothing. If the shares move up 6.5 points, the buyer of an at-the-money call option is on the verge of making money. It is likely that the option will be exercised, leaving the seller with premium income as a bonus plus the agreed strike price. That may or may not be profitable, depending on the price at which the original shares were bought.

It is possible that the option seller may not have profited to any great degree if the shares were originally bought somewhat above the strike price. The option premium certainly is welcome and helps offset the loss. However, the shares may be called away just as they were beginning to show a profit. After all the analysis and selection, which may well be the hardest part of the financial scene, the investment decision could be short-circuited for the sake of a small profit from premium income. It is indeed best to sell options when you have a substantial profit in the shares and do not expect any substantial gain in price.

Once the call seller has sold an option and receives the income, a few choices become available. The option can run its course without any significant change in price of the underlying shares. If the original shares were bought at $50 and the exercise price is also $50, the writer has taken in $6.50 in premiums. The option expires worthless, the writer is 13 percent richer for the six-month option period and the original shares are still in the portfolio, showing neither a loss nor a gain (except for the premium income).

If the underlying shares of the ABC Corporation had moved higher during the contract, they would have been called away. If the buyer of the option had paid $6.50, the option begins to gain value at $56.50. At that price, or higher, it pays to exercise the option if the buyer wants to acquire the shares.

Regardless of the price of the underlying shares, the writer or seller of the option would only be paid $50 per share when the option is exercised. If your original purpose was to sell an option for additional income and some downside protection, you should have no regrets. With the premium income the shares could have fallen to $43.50 before you would show a loss. If the price of the shares moved to $65 or $70, as you originally thought when you bought them, you might feel aggrieved and cheated. Thus, writing the option has not served you well.

Since options, like stocks, are continually traded, you could make other choices as trends developed. If the price of the shares started to rise, you could end the obligation by buying the same option back. No doubt this would be more expensive than the premium first received, but then the original shares are kept. There is nothing to stop the seller from writing another option, at a higher price, thus offsetting some of the higher price paid for buying the call back.

The seller of options may decide to write puts. This might be considered the more speculative side of option writing. In this case, the writer receives premium income for obligating himself to buy stock from someone who thinks the price is headed south. The writer is betting that the option buyer of the put is wrong and that the shares will not fall but instead appreciate. If that is so, why not take money from someone's misperception of market forces?

On the other side, the put writer may view the strategy as conservative rather than speculative. Since the company in question is worthwhile owning, why not try to acquire it cheaply? On top of that, you are receiving money to do just that, a fact that lowers your cost basis.

If you write a put on the ABC Corporation at $50 when it was trading at $50, you would receive the premium, say $6.50. The stock does indeed decline to $45 and the put holder exercises the option. You are now obligated to buy the shares at $50, but the premium has reduced your cost basis to $43.50. If you thought it a tempting buy at $50, it is certainly on sale at $43.50.

If you were wrong, the price of the stock went up and the value of the option goes down. Since there is a continuous market in listed options, you can extricate yourself by buying a put to unwind your position before the option is exercised. This closing transaction cancels out your previous position.

FIGURE 4.1   Comparison of Selling Calls and Puts on Newly
Acquired Stock

	Seller of Call Option	*Seller of Put Option*
Initial trade	Buys 100 shares at $50, sells call at 50 for ($6.50) $650	Buys no shares, sells put at 50 for ($6.50) $650
Stock price goes up	Call is exercised, seller receives $650	Put expires, seller receives $650
Stock price falls	Call expires, seller keeps stock at 50 and premium of $650	Put is exercised, seller buys stock at 50 but keeps premium of $650
Benefits	Keeps dividends until exercised	Lower capital required
Disadvantages	Higher capital required	No dividends

There is not much difference between selling calls or puts on newly acquired stock—you can make as much money one way or the other. Figure 4.1 summarizes the main points.

LEVERAGE EXPLAINED

The major benefit of buying options is summed up in one word: leverage. With options, you get more bang for your buck by skewing the risk-reward relationship. To illustrate the appeal of leverage, compare the results of buying 100 shares of the XYZ Corporation outright and of purchasing a three-month, at-the-money option on the company (Table 4.1).

TABLE 4.1 Comparison of Shares versus Option on XYZ
Corporation

| | Buy 100 Shares @ $30 ($3,000) | | Buy 1 Call Option @ $3 ($300) | |
Price ($)	Profit/Loss	Return (%)	Profit/Loss	Return (%)
30	0	0	–300	– 100
33	+ 300	+ 10	0	0
36	+ 600	+ 20	+300	+ 100
39	+ 900	+ 30	+600	+ 200

The table shows that it is possible to double your money with options while the stock moves only 30 percent. Options are gentler and kinder on the downside: since you never can lose more money than the price of the premium, you will lose 100 percent of your investment. But that may well be only 10 percent of the value of the stock investment, proving that some dark clouds do indeed have a silver lining.

The disadvantage is equally clear: once you have lost 100 percent of the option and it expires, there is no way to recoup. The shares may well fall in half, but they may subsequently recover some if not all of that loss.

Leverage is also present in the price of the premium. Most options are bought at the money. However, there is a powerful speculative incentive for buying shares out of the money. Table 4.2 is a sample of the options tables found in the daily business section of the newspaper.

In June, the 30 August call option has two months to expiration, but with the share prices at $25, there is not much likelihood that the price will move into the $30 range. Therefore, there is no intrinsic value to the option since it is out of the money. The call may be obtained for $75, a reflection of the option's time value.

TABLE 4.2   Sample Options Table

Option & NY Close	Strike Price	Calls-Last			Puts-Last		
		Jun	Jul	Aug	Jun	Jul	Aug
XYZ	20	r	5 3/4	5 7/8	r	r	3/16
25	22 1/2	3	3 1/4	4	r	1/8	1/2
25	25	9/16	1 3/8	2 5/16	3/16	11/16	1 3/8
25	30	r	3/16	3/4	r	r	4 3/4

Note: r = no trades.

Nevertheless, if a speculator believed that some event would immediately increase the company's value when revealed (e.g., a patent approval, a leveraged buyout, the sale of an important asset to raise cash or an extraordinary spurt in earnings) the value of the option would skyrocket. For example, the June 15 call on Time Corporation was trading at 8 3/4 ($875) when the shares were changing hands at $121 per share. The option had only a few weeks to run when Paramount (the old Gulf & Western) made a tender offer of $175 per share. The option rose to $56 overnight, for a gain of $47 ($4,700).

The put side reflects the same leverage for an out-of-the-money option. The August 30 trading at 4 3/4 ($475) in Table 4.2 is at the money, but the August 20 is 3/16 ($18.75). Intimations of disaster would greatly increase the value of the put. If a dramatic drop in sales materialized, the company's shares would nose-dive. For example, the Ashton Tate 22 1/2 put option with one month to expire jumped from 1 1/16 ($106.25) to 4 1/4 ($425) when the company surprisingly announced lower-than-expected earnings for the previous quarter.

Most out of the money calls or puts expire without such dramatic turnarounds. However, for the speculative minded, buying such options provides great potential for profit without putting up great sums of money.

Y•O•U•R   M•O•V•E

- The popularity of common stock options stems from their speculative appeal. They allow you to participate in the fortunes of a corporation for a limited amount of time for a fixed premium. The right to buy or sell a stock option can be had for about 5 or 10 percent of the underlying value of the shares.

- By buying a call option, you control 100 shares of the underlying stock for a short period of time—usually three or six months. You will profit by selling the option at a higher price or by exercising the option if it is in the money. This means that the price of the shares not only exceeds the strike price but also covers the cost of the premium. An in-the-money call option is a way of acquiring shares cheaply.

- By buying a put option, you are betting that the price of the underlying shares will go down in value. The put option allows you to sell a number of shares at a stated price before the contract expires. You profit by either selling the option that has risen in price or by exercising the option to receive the difference between the lower market price and the higher strike price.

- If you do not exercise the option (or sell it before the expiration date), you stand to lose only the price of the premium. This limiting of risk has great appeal to option players.

- For a greater degree of speculation, you might consider selling options—without owning or wanting to own the underlying shares. This "naked" trading can be dangerous to your financial health. While you obtain the premium income from the option buyer, if the market moves the wrong way, you may be forced to sell shares you do not have or buy shares you cannot afford. Selling options is risky since you have an open-ended exposure.

• Unlike other forms of speculating, no credit is involved in option trading. You need not put up margin money or open a special account. The leverage of controlling a lot of stock for a little money is short-lived since the contract expires in a matter of months.

• To be a successful option trader, select options on securities that are likely to show substantial price movement in a relatively brief time. Volatility, regardless of the reason, is the friend of the option speculator.

S • H • O • R • T • C • U • T

Option Mutual Funds

The following option funds write covered options on at least half of their portfolios. (See Chapter 6 "Shortcut" for additional funds.)

• Analytic Option Equity
• Franklin Premier Return
• MIM Mutual: Stock Income
• Shearson Income: Option

• 5 •

Options: Other Choices

Common stock options have been extremely popular since their inception. No doubt their success has stimulated the financial world to look for other option vehicles. Many more types of options were created in the early 1980s. While the option principle remains the same, these new options are more complicated to understand since they deal with abstractions such as debt, indexes and stock index futures.

To be clear about the relationships of these derivative instruments, remember that there are four possible markets for all financial instruments:

1. The *cash market* is one in which investors and speculators buy (or sell) stocks or bonds. The quality of these instruments determines whether they are investments or speculations.
2. *Options on the cash market,* as discussed in Chapter 4, are best illustrated by the popularity of options on common stock. An option gives you a limited right for a premium payment to buy a cash instrument, such as a common stock.
3. The *futures markets* were discussed in Chapter 3. A futures contract allows you to speculate on a commodity, debt obligation or stock index for a small down payment.

4. *Options on the futures market* give you a limited right to obtain control over a futures contract.

In general, the more derivative the instrument, or the more removed from the underlying instrument, the more speculative and volatile it is likely to be.

Besides common stock, there are options on five types of financial instruments: (1) debt instruments, (2) stock indexes, (3) foreign currencies, (4) precious metals and (5) agricultural commodities.

As seen in Chapter 3, there is an active market in short-term and long-term government paper, from T-bonds to T-bills, Eurodollars, certificates of deposit and Ginnie Maes. The price of the underlying debt instrument is the final determinant of the value of the debt option.

Short-term debt instruments (sometimes known as money market instruments) have maturities of less than one year. They are generally quoted in terms of rates or yield from which their price must be determined. Bonds, on the other hand, are quoted in terms of dollar prices, from which their yields must be determined. Options, however, are priced in dollars to arrive at exercise prices. (To convert rate or yield changes into price changes, see Chapter 2 of *The Basics of Bonds.*)

If you want to speculate in debt instrument options, always remember that the debt market turns on the inverse relationship of rate to principal: when interest rates go up, the price of the principal falls, and vice versa.

Call options become more valuable and puts less valuable as prices increase (when yields are falling); puts become more valuable and calls less valuable as prices decline (when yields are rising). In brief, you must factor in the interest rate's effect on fixed interest securities. This is an additional step, but it is a critical one if you are not to find yourself on the wrong side of what you originally intended.

Debt options have a number of uses, but they are primarily a hedge against interest rate changes. They can be used to protect a bond portfolio (if interest rates move up) by buying a put option. Or debt options might be written against a portfolio of bonds or other fixed income securities that do not in themselves have debt options.

Therefore, if you want to protect your long position against an interest rate increase (and a price decrease), purchase a put option (which locks in a selling price) or sell a call option. If you anticipate an interest rate decline (and a price increase), purchase a call option (which locks in a purchase price) or sell a put.

If you wish to speculate, reverse the process. Since you have no position to protect, if you anticipate an interest rate increase (and a price decrease), sell a put option or buy a call option. And if you anticipate an interest rate decline (and a price increase), sell a call option or buy a put.

T-BILL AND OTHER
SHORT-TERM INTEREST RATE OPTIONS

Treasury bill call options (and other short-term interest rate instruments options) can be used to hedge against a decline in money market interest rates and thus safeguard a set rate of return. T-bill put options might be purchased by a borrower to hedge any lender's interest rate that varies with the prime rate. The same strategy might be used to hedge a variable rate mortgage by buying options on Ginnie Maes. While these hedging devices protect an investor's interest rate liabilities, there is no reason why a speculator cannot also buy and/or sell options on debt instruments either for appreciation or income.

While the T-bill market is extraordinarily broad and deep, the T-bill option market is relatively thin and small.

For the most part, it is not a market for individual investors or speculators of moderate means since the options are on $1 million positions. Moreover, the T-bill option, with its short duration, does not lend itself as an adequate hedge in the circumstances previously mentioned. Individual speculators are better served in the T-bond option market.

CAN YOU HEDGE LONG-TERM INTEREST RATES: T-BOND OPTIONS

The most popular of the options on debt instruments are those on bonds and notes. T-bond options trade daily in thousands of contracts. They are less complex than T-bill options, and they trade in smaller contracts—$100,000 principal amounts. These options are for a specific issue, and that issue must be delivered, not just any $100,000 T-bond.

At any time, several issues will be trading, but options on issues are traded only for a while since liquidity tends to dry up on the underlying securities. Therefore, trading interest is keenest on newly auctioned issues. As a consequence, a full range of options expirations are not usually available.

Happily, exercise prices for bonds and note options are expressed in the same fashion as in the cash market—a percentage of par value. If the exercise price is 92 for the holder of the call, it entitles the holder to purchase the bond for $92,000 plus accrued interest on the bond since it was last paid. A speculator is not likely to exercise the option but will sell it if it is in the money.

Exercise prices are fixed at levels then prevailing in the market for the underlying security. Higher and lower exercise prices are introduced as market prices fluctuate.

Premiums are expressed in terms of points and 64ths, with each 1/64 representing 1/64 of 1 percent of the principal amount trading. Thus, a premium of 3 16/64 indicates that the price is $3,250.

Along with stocks and futures, these options expire quarterly, on the third Friday of the expiration month. Some options are quite long, with durations of 15 months; thus they are ideal for hedging long-term debt. Unlike T-bill options, no adjustment to price has to be made for delivery in the event of exercised options.

WILL OPTIONS ON
FUTURES LIMIT YOUR RISK?

With the introduction of options on financial futures contracts, the commodity exchanges have squared the circle, so to speak. We have examined the cash market; the trading of U.S. government bills, notes and bonds; the futures market to hedge long and short positions in Treasury paper; the options market on debt instruments (options on "actuals") to benefit from or protect against changes in interest rates; and finally, an option market on financial futures.

For speculators, options on futures limit the open-ended exposure implicit in futures contracts. These derivative instruments (both the options and the futures) are based on the underlying issues, whether they be commodities (i.e., agricultural and other physicals) or interest rate instruments. When you buy or sell a futures contract, you take on a contractual obligation that is not ended until you close out the other side of the transaction (or take or make delivery of the commodity in question).

The volatility of commodity markets and the great leverage connected with these contracts makes them either highly profitable or a danger to your wealth. Remember, in a T-bond futures contract where the principal amount is $100,000, a speculator is obliged to put up $3,000 for initial margin. The daily limit move is 96/32nds or $3,000. The whole principal (or more) can be erased in minutes or in a few days since one-point moves in the bond market are not that uncommon.

Is there a way to protect yourself from the vagaries of price fluctuation but still be a player? The options on futures are the answer. As with all options, your risk is limited to the price of the premium. Moreover, options are not marked to the market every day; therefore, a sharp downdraft (which would wipe you out in the futures) may well be followed by an equally sharp recovery. Your position remains intact until the expiration date of the option, though the price of it will vary.

Options on interest rate futures have multiple uses. Most speculators buy and sell the option to establish capital gains. However, it is possible to exercise the option and acquire the futures contract if you are long and in the money. The option expires in the month prior to the settlement month of the futures contract (e.g., March T-bond options expire in February). While most traders prefer to make their money on options, it is possible to take possession of the futures contract for the few remaining weeks to settlement. At that point, another decision must be made about how to close out the futures contract. Of course, once you exercise the option and acquire the futures, you then are assuming the open-ended liability inherent in futures trading.

The basic strategy for both instruments is the same: buying a call option is appropriate if you anticipate a decrease in interest rates, and an option on a futures contract enables you to buy a long futures contract at the option exercise price. On the other hand, if you anticipate an increase in interest rates, buying a put option would be the right move, and the exercise of a put option on a futures contract will give you a short position in the futures contract at the exercise price, that is, the sale of the futures contract.

It is clear that speculators in the option market have two parallel markets: the options on interest rate instruments and the options on the futures. The former is regulated by the Securities and Exchange Commission (SEC), and the latter is regulated by the Commodity Futures Trading Commission(CFTC), even though the underlying securities are the same.

While that difference is not important to the individual investor, the debt option market is more difficult to track than the futures market since it is more of a dealer market with the traditional bid-and-ask arrangement. Future options prices are derived from a continuous open outcry system that is employed in the commodity trading pits to provide greater liquidity. Moreover, prices are published daily and are readily available.

Perhaps the major difference between the options on futures and the futures themselves is that the option limits the risk, but at the price of the premium, which is not negligible. Premiums on T-bond contracts may range between $2,000 and $4,000, depending on option dates. If the market does not move, this option instrument is a wasting asset. The seller, of course, faces a loss if the market goes in the wrong direction but does not face a serious loss until the premium income is eroded. The holder of a futures contract is faced with the risk that the price might move too much—and the wrong way. If the market remains static and goes nowhere, the speculator loses only a small commission fee, $22 to $100, which is far less than the premium for the option.

WHY IS INDEX TRADING SO POPULAR?

You can take a position in an index at any time, for any length of time, and you don't need a wheelbarrow of money. In short, index trading in options, futures and futures options is now one of the chief ways of speculating in the stock market.

Developed in the early 1980s, these indexes have achieved enormous popularity. Though exploited and widely used by institutional money managers, portfolio insurers, arbitrageurs, banks, pension funds and their ilk, they are also a great boon to the small investor or speculator.

In one instrument, indexes provide a portfolio with the diversification that someone with limited resources might not be able to afford. In one instrument, you can buy or sell the whole market. This is highly attractive to market participants who are better at sensing market trends and directions than they are at picking individual issues.

Indexes are, of course, nothing new, but their use as surrogates for the market is relatively recent. Different indexes give different market perspectives, but there is rather remarkable uniformity in the major moves that they trace. There is a wide assortment of indexes, but for the purposes of general trading, only the significant ones will be examined.

The granddaddy of market indicators is the Dow Jones Industrial Average, but that gauge of 30 of America's largest corporations is not used in index trading because of legal proprieties. Equally famous is Standard & Poor's 100 (an index of 100 blue-chip companies) and Standard & Poor's 500 (industrials, utilities, financials and transportation companies). Both are weighted by market capitalization; that is, each company's price is multiplied by its shares outstanding and is then averaged. The base figure of 10 for the Standard & Poor's 500 was established in 1943, while the Standard & Poor's 100 started in 1976.

Index trading also uses the New York Stock Exchange Composite Index, which provides a daily average of the price changes of about 1,500 common stocks traded on the New York Stock Exchange. This is also a weighted average (the base of 50 was established in 1965); the largest companies have the greatest proportional impact. The American Stock Exchange has the Major Market Index, a reflection of the leading blue chips. The Value Line Index is a geometric average of 1,700 companies listed on the New York and American Stock Exchanges: it has a 1969 base of 100, but it measures percentage changes rather than dollar values. The Value Line Index is somewhat more sensitive to change.

These are the major indexes for index trading, but others exist for more specialized purposes. New indexes are constantly being developed, though their life spans are sometimes brief. If you are considering speculating in this area, do so with popular and well-tried vehicles.

Unlike stock options (which are settled by the delivery of stock) or options on futures (which are settled with futures contracts), options on indexes are settled in cash. To see how that works, let's examine the Standard & Poor's (S&P) 100 (OEX) options traded on the Chicago Board. A holder of an index option that is in the money receives the difference between the strike or exercise price and the index value at the close of the exercise day. With OEX, the multiple is 100 (as compared to 500 for the S&P 500 or the NYSE Composite Index).

To illustrate, suppose you expect a general bull market move. You buy one six-month call option at 245 (when the S&P 100 index is at 250) for a premium of $10, or $1,000. Three months later the S&P 100 index has gained 14 points, closing at 264, and you decide to exercise. This is how to calculate your profit:

Dollar value:	$26,400
(264 × 1 × $100)	
Less:	
Aggregate exercise price	
(245 × 1 × $100)	24,500
Gross settlement	$ 1,900
Less: Premium ($10 × 1)	1,000
Net profit	$ 900

It is not necessary to exercise the option to realize a profit. The more usual way is simply to sell the option, since the price would have appreciated in parallel fashion. The worst thing that could have happened would have been a loss of the premium (the $1,000) if the market had retreated or remained static. The option buyer, however, would bail out if his or her assumptions proved to be wrong before the time value of the option had completely vanished.

The OEX is the most popular option, with 100,000 to 150,000 calls and puts trading daily. Thus, a speculator can participate for a few hundred dollars on either side of the market. If you have a larger appetite, you can either buy a number of OEX options or move up to the S&P 500 (SPX), where the multiplier is not 100 but 500. And speculators with an interest for income can, of course, sell options. Since you cannot, in practice, make or take delivery of the underlying shares, the margin regulations for option writers are somewhat more complicated than stock options. (For exact details consult your broker.)

STOCK INDEX FUTURES

The second index trading vehicles of note are the stock index futures. You can buy (or sell) a futures contract that is tied to one of the major indexes—the S&P 500, the NYSE Composite, the Major Market, the Value Line or the Commodity Research Bureau (CRB), which is based on commodity components. All of these contracts have a multiplier of 500, except for the small Major Market, which has a multiplier of 250.

Stock index contracts are similar to other financial futures, except that no commodity is delivered upon settlement, only cash. To take a position, you must make a minimum deposit in a commodity account. This is only a good-faith deposit, but considering the face value of the S&P 500 futures (500 × index), when the index is at 325, the face value is $162,500. Therefore, the initial deposit of $15,000 is not insignificant: indeed, because of their large multipliers, these futures indexes require more of a down payment than any other commodity.

The S&P 500 futures are the most popular of the index futures and are carefully watched for both their predictive nature and their arbitrage possibilities for institutions in program trading. If you bought a futures contract yesterday at the opening, you would read a report similar to the one in Table 5.1 in your morning paper.

By the close of the day you lost $1,325 (2.65 × 500). In this contract the minimum fluctuation is 0.05, or $25. If the contract reached the life of the contract high, 328.45, and was then sold, there would be a gain of 2.85, or $1,425 (2.85 × 500). If the market crashed (a worst case scenario) and the low was taken out, you might have lost 61.80, a

TABLE 5.1   S&P 500 Index (CME) 500 Times Index

Open	High	Low	Settle	Chg	High	Low	Open Interest
325.60	325.90	323.15	324.15	−2.65	328.45	263.80	66,711

devastating $30,900 (61.80 × 500) if no stop orders were there for protection.

S&P 500 index futures are based on the S&P 500 composite stock index and naturally reflect its movements. However, the two are not quite identical. If you want to own the stock portfolio represented by the index, you must make a large capital outlay, although you do receive dividends. Buying the index futures ties up relatively little capital. The difference in price between the actual portfolio and the index futures is accounted for by a difference between the dividend yield of the former and the investment yield on the residual funds left over from buying the futures contract. Transaction costs are also considerably higher for stocks than for futures, which also separates the two valuations.

FOR SOPHISTICATED SPECULATORS: OPTIONS ON STOCK INDEX FUTURES

The final index trading instruments are options on stock index futures. We have previously examined options on the stock indexes; these are options on the futures. These options, similar to debt options, differ only in that the option buyer receives a futures contract based on a stock index if the option is exercised. The one with the most volume is the S&P 500 Stock Index, which is traded on the Chicago Mercantile Exchange. Most option buyers do not take delivery of the futures contract but settle in cash by selling the option, especially if the option is in the money.

Remember that the option's protection ends when the option holder takes delivery of the futures option. Since the S&P 500 has a 500 multiplier, the futures contract is one of the largest in the futures market. Moreover, the premium on the option is not times 100 but times 500 as well. The other futures option is on the NYSE Composite Index, with a 500 multiplier, though the index is little more than half of the S&P index.

The option gives the holder the right, but not the obligation, to take a position at the strike price of the S&P 500. For example, Table 5.2 appears in the financial pages.

If you bought the S&P 320 June call option, you would pay a premium of (4.65 × 500) $2,325. If you exercise, a position is taken in the underlying S&P futures contract at 320—a long position. If it was a put option, you would establish a short position at 320. If you wrote the option, then you must take a short position in the futures contract, while a put writer is obliged to take a long position. Once a position in a futures contract is taken, margin or earnest money must be deposited. Of course, you had to deposit margin when the option was initiated.

How do you determine if the option is profitable? It is clear that if the market moves in the right direction, the option's value will appreciate. If the option expires, a cash settlement is made on the closing level of the index, which is the difference between the option strike price and the closing level of the index. If the index closes at 320.75, then the call is valued at $375 (.75 × 500), slightly in the money.

TABLE 5.2   S&P 500 Stock Index Options (CME), $500 Times Premium

Strike Price	Calls-Settle			Puts-Settle		
	Jun-c	Jly-c	Sp-c	Jun-p	Jly-p	Sp-p
315	9.25	15.55	18.50	0.10	2.05	5.20
320	4.65	11.55	15.05	0.50	3.05	6.65
325	1.40	8.15	11.95	2.25	4.60	8.45
Close	323.91					

In the final analysis, it is up to the trader to determine whether the option on the futures or the futures is a better bet. Options provide predetermined risk, but this risk limitation commands a hefty price in the premium. Futures leave one exposed to risk, but then the entrance fee, the commission, was negligible. Profits in the futures will probably exceed profits in the options, but then again so will the losses.

Y·O·U·R   M·O·V·E

- Besides common stock options, it is possible to speculate on debt instruments. With common stock options, you are evaluating the prospects of a corporation. With debt options, you are making a decision on the direction of interest rates. Choose the option that best suits the economic environment: stock options when the equity markets are booming; debt options when interest rates are volatile.

- Make sure that you appreciate how the inverse relationship of interest rate to principal effects the debt option. When yields fall, call options increase in value, and puts increase but to a lesser degree. When yields rise, you want to own the put and sell the call.

- T-bond options are most commonly used to hedge and speculate. The $100,000 contract can be controlled for a few thousand dollars of premium. A small move in interest rates can exert great pressure on the premium. You profit from these options when interest rates are in flux.

- Remember that when you exercise an option on a futures contract, you are obliged to take possession of a futures position (whether long or short). You are then assuming an open-ended exposure in the commodity, be it an agricultural commodity or an interest rate instrument. If you are averse to great risk, stay with the option.

• If you have a strong sense of market direction, you can capitalize on that talent by trading index options. In volatile markets these options can be quite profitable, or they can show significant losses—sometimes both in the course of one day. For more aggressive speculation, you might try stock index futures or options on stock index futures. The futures must be monitored closely if you are to avoid margin calls.

S • H • O • R • T • C • U • T

Leveraged Mutual Funds

Some mutual funds use borrowed funds to increase their return on investment. This leverage may be used with stocks, bonds, futures or options. Leveraged funds tend to be more volatile than funds that use no borrowed cash.

• American Heritage
• Dreyfus Strategic
• Morgan Grenfill Small Cap
• Prudent Speculator
• Value Line Leveraged Growth

• 6 •

Option Strategies

TACTICS FOR HEDGING
AND SPECULATING

The range and diversity of options is staggering: you can deal with options on common stocks, debt instruments, debt futures, indexes and stock index futures. Each type of option on a specific instrument has a special purpose. However, the use of options falls into two categories as options are used as hedging vehicles or speculating vehicles.

In the first category—managing a portfolio—an investor owns the underlying securities and wishes to hedge the position. Therefore, by buying or selling options an investor is hedging against risk. Selling options provides additional income to raise the rate of return of a portfolio.

In the second category, options as speculative vehicles offer liquidity and high leverage. They offer the possibility of large profits for relatively small sums and enable traders to speculate on volatility, with or without determining the direction of a market. It is this second category that most directly appeals to speculators.

There are a number of strategies for speculators—many of them too complex to explain in this introductory book. In any event, the best strategies are perhaps the simplest and most forthright.

FIGURE 6.1   Buy a Call

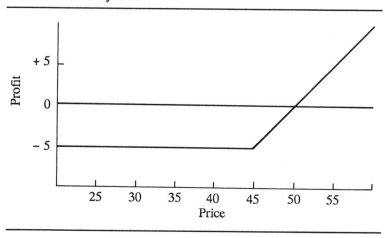

There are many option combinations, both for hedging and speculating, whether you are in the bull or bear camp. The graphs in Figures 6.1 through 6.7 illustrate some of the basic option strategies with which a speculator should be familiar.

With a strike price of $45, the buyer of a call does not begin to profit until the underlying security exceeds 50 when the premium is $5 (see Figure 6.1). In short, a break-even point for the buyer of a call is the exercise price plus the option premium. If the issue rises to $55, the call buyer doubles his or her initial investment.

Some speculators sell or write naked calls, that is, they are uncovered because they maintain no long position in the security. They keep all of the option premium, $5 ($5 × 100 = $500). This is profitable if the price of the issue does not rise above the break-even point, the $45 strike price, plus the $5 call premium, or $50 (see Figure 6.2).

Buying a put (Figure 6.3) is the reverse of buying a call. The price of the issue must decline below the strike price for it to be profitable to the put buyer. In this case, the put

FIGURE 6.2   Sell or Write a Call

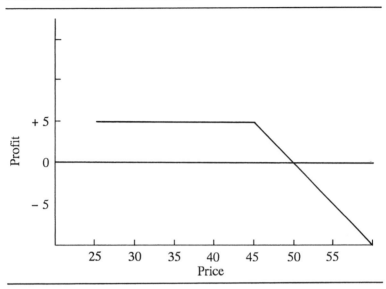

is profitable below $40 (the strike price of $45 minus the option premium).

The speculator who sells naked puts is fully exposed to the market. In return, the seller receives all of the put premium if the issue is selling at or above the strike price when the option expires. The option's profitability falls as the price falls below the strike price. The put seller starts to lose money when the price falls below $45 (see Figure 6.4).

If a trader expects a violent market but is uncertain which direction the breakout will go, a straddle may be his or her answer. A *straddle* is the purchase of a put and a call—two options with identical strike prices. You can, of course, lose both premiums if the stock remains relatively fixed at the strike price so that the exercise of either option does not justify the commission. Since this is unlikely, it is hard to lose the total premium. It is also hard to profit since one option is bound to expire worthless within the expira-

FIGURE 6.3   Buy a Put

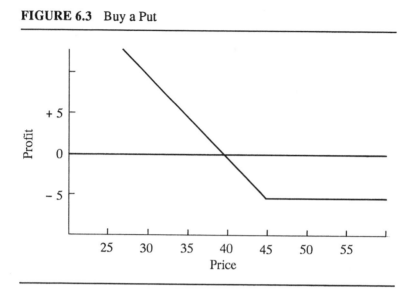

tion period. The other option has to move dramatically before the straddle buyer can recover the premium and begin to profit.

In Figure 6.5 the break-even point on the upside is the strike price, $45, plus the $5 put premium, plus the $5 call premium, or $55. On the downside, the break-even point

FIGURE 6.4   Sell or Write a Put

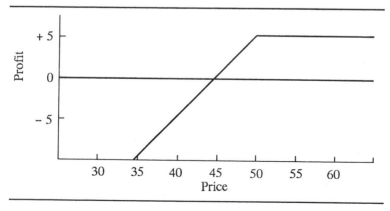

FIGURE 6.5 Buy a Straddle

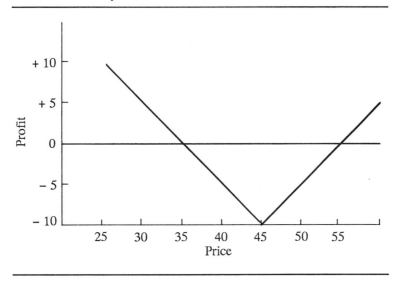

is the strike price, $45, minus the $5 put premium, minus the $5 call premium, or $35.

Selling naked straddles appeals to speculators since it recognizes one of the basic facts of market life: often the market does not move in any substantial way. This is the opposite strategy of the straddle buyer who expects a disruptive move one way or another. Maximum profitability comes when the striking prices of the options are identical—at that point neither side of the straddle will be exercised. When the price moves away from the strike price, the profit to the naked writer declines. The seller earns a profit from $35 on the low side to $55 on the high side (see Figure 6.6). To maintain a profit, the seller hopes that when the straddle expires the issue price is dead center, or at least between the two parameters.

Market participants should be familiar with what has become the most popular of all option strategies—writing a covered call. This is not a speculator's most aggressive stance; however, for anyone thinking about options, it is

FIGURE 6.6   Sell a Straddle

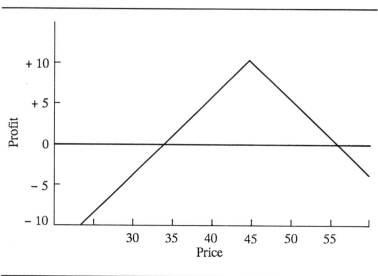

worth considering. The strategy is simple: buy the underlying security and sell a call using the issue as collateral.
The premium income gives protection: the $5 premium will
provide downside protection to $45 for the issues pur-
chased at $50 (see Figure 6.7). But there is a tradeoff. The
covered-call writer's profit is capped since once the option
is in the money, the option buyer will exercise the right to
buy. It is clear that if the underlying issue moves ahead
strongly, the covered-call writer would have been better off
not writing the call. A covered-call writer could also write
a put if the market looked like it was heading south. That
move would afford the same premium income and protection to a portfolio position.

This buy-write strategy has a number of applications.
It provides some additional income. It also provides some
downside protection against a long position that, if sold,
might have high tax consequences. The option seller can
deliver newly bought shares instead of the old shares to
avoid capital gains tax. This option strategy can be used if

FIGURE 6.7   Purchase the Stock and Sell a Call

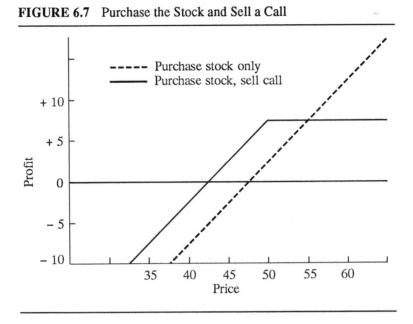

the option premium is overpriced; hence, it is attractive to a writer.

There are a number of other option combinations. By and large, the more complicated option strategies are used to protect portfolios from market risk. That is not a primary consideration for those who are speculatively inclined.

SOME BULL STRATEGIES

Buy a Call Option

The option speculator finds an attractive option, one with volatility and a reasonable premium. In return for the premium, a successful option buyer will be paid off at execution point for point with the rise in price of the underlying instrument once this price is above the strike price. If the option expires out of the money, then the speculator has lost the entire premium. In general, the higher the strike price of a call option, the lower the premium. Traders are inclined to buy calls that are just slightly out of the money. This strategy is one of the purest speculative plays, but some speculators are more cautious and use spreads.

A *spread* is the simultaneous initiation of opposite positions. There are different kinds of spreads (sometimes they are called straddles when the same exercise price and same expiration dates are used), but the logic is to establish a relationship between two different options. There are various ways of accomplishing this. The purchase of one option and the sale of another option on the same security is the simplest way. A speculator hopes to profit from a change in the difference between the prices of the two options. In other words, the trader is less concerned with absolute values than with price differentials. A second bullish strategy is to execute a bull spread, that is, to purchase the call option and sell a call option.

Long Call Option and Short Call Option

This strategy provides protection on both sides. It is done on the expectation of unusual volatility, but the trader is uncertain of the direction in which the breakout will move. The spread is established by buying one option contract and selling another on the same issue but at different exercise prices or maturities. (A vertical spread occurs when both options have the same expiration date but different strike prices. In a time spread, both options have the same exercise price, but they have different expiration months.)

For example, the ABC Company is selling at $42 per share. A trader who expects an important move buys the in-the-money call for six months at $40 for a premium of $500. If the price dramatically appreciates, the profit on the option starts at $45 and moves concurrently with the price of the underlying shares. If the stock does not move, the $500 premium is lost. By selling a six-month option on the issue at $50 for $250 of premium income, the trader has two positions, for a cost of $250 ($500 − $250). In other words, the most that can be lost is $250—the difference between the prices of the two options.

On the downside, a trader expects a sharp decline in ABC from $90 a share. To profit, an in-the-money call is written at $80 for a premium of $1,200. If the price of ABC declines to $79 at the exercise time, the profit will be $700—the difference between the two premiums. If the price had not declined, the maximum loss would be $300 (the $1,000 difference between the exercise prices of the two options less the net premium of $700). Had the $90 call not been purchased, the speculator's exposure to loss would have been unlimited.

This strategy may offer a profit, but the covered call also limits profit potential by the nature of the contradictory price movements. If the long position call is sold at a profit when share prices advance, the short call's premium value has simultaneously shrunk. Most spreads are not exercised, but if that happens to one leg of the exercise, the spread is destroyed. If the short call was exercised, it can be met by delivering stock already owned or by buying stock in the market, borrowing stock or exercising the call option.

This bull spread has the effect of trading off some upside gain in exchange for a reduction in the net up-front premium. The same logic applies to spreads in commodities and financial futures. By taking positions in opposing directions in related items, the speculator hopes to profit from an expected change in the relationship between the purchase price of one and the selling price of the other. Whether you sell March wheat contracts and buy May wheat contracts or take a long position in March Treasury bonds and a short position in June Treasury bonds, the expectation is similar: you hope to profit by the expansion or contraction between the spread contracts.

SOME BEAR STRATEGIES

On the other side of the coin, there are two basic bearish strategies: (1) the long put and (2) the bear spread. They are mirror reflections of the bullish strategies.

Buy a Put Option

A trader who believes that the market is overpriced and consequently due for a fall might buy a put option rather than short the market since it ties up less money, limits loss to the price of the premium, avoids margin calls if the market moves the wrong way and creates no obligation to cover if the market advances. The put gives the buyer the right to sell at a specific (lower) price at any time during the life of the option. To succeed, the trader needs a volatile option vehicle, enough time for the expectation to be fulfilled and a premium that is reasonably priced.

Once the price of the underlying security falls below the strike price, the buyer's profit moves point for point with the underlying issue. If the put option expires out of the money, the trader will lose the total premium. In general, the lower the strike price, the lower the option premium. For speculators, the purchase of a put option is one of the purest ways of using leverage in a bear market. For the put writer, the premium income provides some cushion if the put is exercised. The put writer is not speculatively inclined but is merely looking for additional income and/or the chance of buying issues cheaply.

Long Put Option and Short Put Option

This combination spread of a long put option and a short put option with a lower exercise price is known as a *bear spread*. It is the opposite of the bull spread: its intention is to reduce the net premium cost of owning a long option position by selling a second, out-of-the-money option that sacrifices some of the profit potential of the first option.

For instance, when a stock is at $50, buy a $40 put for $750 while simultaneously selling a put at $50 for $375. The maximum loss is the difference between the price of the two options ($750 − $375), or $375. If the price does fall, the profit on the long put is offset by the short put. However, the long put option in the money gained value point for point with the decline, but the value of the short put was diminished.

WHAT TO LOOK FOR IN OPTIONS

The traditional wisdom in the options world is to "sell overpriced options and buy underpriced options." Easier said than done! However, the speculator must examine the components of all options to decide whether an option is overpriced or underpriced and whether a trade is likely to be profitable. You must examine the intrinsic value of an option (the market price of the security plus or minus the striking price of its option) as well as its time value.

Moreover, you must do some comparison shopping: how are other comparable options priced? Comparison pricing should give you some reasonable grounds for evaluating whether an option is overpriced or underpriced.

A major consideration in the premium is the strike price. In-the-money, at-the-money or out-of-the-money strike prices naturally have different costs attached to them. The cheapest premium is out of the money since the possibility of exercise is remote. Out-of-the-money options can be most rewarding for speculators. They are particularly appealing if one has some advance information that will dramatically alter an issue's price, such as a labor walkout, a management leveraged buyout or an impending drought.

At-the-money options are the second most expensive, while in-the-money options are the most costly. For the seller, the most profitable is the at-the-money option, while the out-of-the-money brings in the least income. However, the out-of-the-money calls are likely to be the most profitable to write.

Since options are wasting assets, their value depreciates every day. Therefore, a long option of six months has twice as much time value as an option of three months. Longer options are more costly than short ones, but option players should calculate time value on a daily basis to make sure they are getting their money's worth. Long options are more expensive, but they are often cheaper to own on a pro rata basis. An out-of-the-money call for 90 days may be priced at 2 5/8, whereas the 180-day call is priced at 4 1/2: the latter is thus cheaper than the former.

Finally, option players must consider the volatility of the underlying issue. Conservative stocks may show little fluctuation, but options on stock indexes can be extraordinarily vulnerable to price fluctuation. Speculators and call buyers in general wish for volatile times, which is the opposite desire of prudent portfolio managers and option writers.

Issues perceived to be volatile are expensive, that is, they are usually overpriced since grantors of such options demand high premiums. And the public is frequently willing to overpay option writers, especially on hot issues or those that have caught the spotlight. Nevertheless, speculators should be aware of the observations of Fischer Black and Myron Scholes, who are authorities in option models. They have concluded that options on very volatile stocks are likely to be underpriced while premiums on less volatile stocks are likely to be overpriced.

While there are mathematical models available from varied sources (including your brokerage firm) to indicate volatility and evaluate premiums, the occasional option player can consult daily publications to see where an option is trading with regard to its high-low parameters. Once an option moves above the average or median price, it becomes increasingly overpriced. Of course, options tend to lose value as the exercise period expires, regardless of the price action of the underlying shares.

Some studies of option players in the equity markets should help all traders develop some perspective as to profitability and the odds of success. First, less than 5 percent of call options are ever exercised. Those that are exercised have acquired shares at below-market prices. Most call options, about 70 percent, are liquidated through offsetting transactions. Many traders in this group will profit by selling their options at higher prices (without having to exercise), and some traders, no doubt, lose some of their premiums, though not necessarily all when they see the trends and the expiration periods running against them. About one-quarter of all options expire worthless.

The figures for put options are rather similar: 80 percent are ended by offsetting transactions, 15 percent expire worthless and only 5 percent are exercised.

Call buyers tend to be the most enthusiastic buyers of options and consequently pay too much. Put buyers are somewhat more realistic since unlike a call, which can appreciate without limit, there is a limit to how far an issue will fall. Finally, it is important to consider commission costs to see if a transaction is indeed profitable.

Y · O · U · R   M · O· V· E

- The best time to buy options is when markets are dull and premiums are cheap. But cheap premiums do not provide enough of a reason to buy options. You must have a concrete reason to believe that some information within the exercise period will strongly move the underlying shares. Options are most costly in bull markets, and calls are proportionately more expensive than puts.

- In-the-money options are less speculative than out-of-the-money options. Out-of-the-money options have the most leverage—you can control the shares for the smallest premium. However, out-of-the-money options have the least chance of being profitable.

- To profit on the sell side, you must sell overpriced options. The best time to sell calls is at the top of markets; and conversely, the time to sell puts is at the bottom.

- Sell out-of-the-money options since the time value is certain to erode the option's value. Profits can be made even before the expiration through an offsetting transaction.

- Since the option market is highly leveraged, you must monitor your positions daily. No margin calls are issued when your position is deteriorating.

S • H • O • R • T • C • U • T

Many mutual funds use puts and calls as a strategy to improve the rate of return, but the bulk of their investments are not in options.

Option Mutual Funds

- Dean Witter Options
- National Premium Income
- Putnam Option
- Oppenheimer Premium Income

• 7 •

Rights and Warrants

CAN YOU SPECULATE WITH PRUDENCE?

One of the small corners of the financial world is the arena of rights and warrants. It is particularly suited to speculators who can use the inherent leverage of these instruments to control far more common stock than their funds would ordinarily allow. Moreover, rights and warrants can significantly increase the rate of return on funds without substantially increasing risk. In addition, they appeal to speculators who are looking for greater volatility in their portfolios.

RIGHTS

Rights (and warrants as well) are not speculative instruments per se. They serve an appropriate function in financing corporations.

Rights are instruments issued by a corporation as a way of raising additional capital. Instead of approaching the general investing public for funds, a corporation offers subscription rights to its current shareholders. Stockholders who purchase these rights can maintain their proportionate share of ownership in the business. Even though the pie gets larger, each shareholder who buys these rights is entitled to the same sized slice. Therefore, the stockholders are said to have a preemptive right to buy a pro rata share of the new issues.

Shareholders can and do sell their rights when they do not wish to subscribe to the new offering. A secondary market will spring into being if there is any public interest in a corporation.

Stockholders are ordinarily offered one right for each share of stock they own, but they may be required to own a number of rights (10 or 20, for example) to subscribe to a single share of the new issue. The board of directors sets a subscription price on the new shares that is somewhat below the current price of the stock in the market. This discount from market value is intended to entice holders to subscribe.

The price of the new shares is set shortly before the issuance, and the rights are likely to exist for only one or two months. Rights can be thought of as short-term call options, but they are initially made available only to stockholders of record as of the date the SEC stamps its approval on an issue.

When the rights are issued, each stockholder of record has the following alternatives: (1) he or she can exercise the rights and subscribe to the stock; (2) he or she can sell the rights in the secondary market; (3) he or she can let the rights expire. Since the rights usually have some monetary value, the last choice is not likely, but about 2 percent of most rights offerings are simply discarded.

The new rights may be traded as soon as the stock goes *ex-rights* (the underlying shares no longer carry the rights privilege) on a when-issued basis. This trading usually lasts only a few days or weeks, until the actual rights are in the stockholders' hands. Listed shares that trade ex-rights may suffer some diminution of value—that is, the value of the rights.

What's a Right Worth?

Many speculators sell rights immediately on a when-issued basis, working on the belief that the first prices for rights are usually the best. Afterwards, the sale of rights by unsubscribing stockholders tends to depress the shares. The "sell rights early" school does not have much evidence to support its contention. A more likely determinant of price is the trend of the underlying shares.

Nevertheless, rights do have a definable value. To determine that value, you must appreciate the arithmetic of the capitalization. If a company has two million common shares outstanding but wishes to issue an additional 100,000 to bring forth more capital, each stockholder will receive one right per share owned. A stockholder must have 20 rights to purchase one new share. (The price of the share—the exercise price—is, of course, lower than the market price. Moreover, shares acquired through a rights offering avoid the cost of a brokerage commission.)

The following formula can be used to figure the value of a right:

$$\frac{\text{Market price of stock} - \text{Subscription price of new stock}}{\text{Number of rights to purchase one share}}$$

Assume the current market price is $30 a share and the new exercise price is $22.50. An investor needs 20 rights to obtain one new share. Thus, the right has the following value:

$$\frac{\$30 - \$22.50}{20} = 0.375$$

If the market price remains about $30, then each right has a value of 37.5 cents: a stockholder with 100 shares has rights worth $37.50. The actual market in the rights will reflect that value, though the oscillating nature of markets will find speculators above and below that price. If the market price moves up to $34 during the course of the rights offering, the rights' price would move up to 57.5 cents.

For the speculator, it is the leverage that is so attractive. In the previous example, the stock moved from $30 to $34, an increase of 13.3 percent. But look at what happened to the rights. They moved from .375 to .575 cents, an increase of 53.3 percent. For this reason, speculators welcome the opportunity to buy rights, especially those that have a longer exercise period.

Shares that are sold ex-rights would, of course, fall in price—a fall equivalent to the value of the rights. If for some reason the common shares fell below the subscription price, the rights would then have no value and the offering would be a disaster. Investors would buy the cheaper stock rather than the rights issue. Prices, however, are usually stabilized by the investment banking firm while an offering is underway.

Speculators are always looking for underpriced rights, especially near the end of an offering, when acquiring the rights is a way of buying subscription shares without a commission. Moreover, even though there are more shares outstanding at the end of an offering, there is often a fillip in the price of the stock when the offering is over.

WARRANTS

Warrants are frequently issued when companies are reorganized, whether because of bankruptcy or some merger. For these reasons, warrants may fluctuate widely as the perceived fortunes of the issuers rise and fall. And it is for this reason that warrants are attractive to speculators.

A *warrant* can be thought of as either an extended right or a long call option. Simply put, a warrant allows its holder to buy the common stock at a fixed price over a fixed period (usually two to ten years), but some warrants are perpetual. Warrants are issued with the sale of preferred stocks or bonds as sweeteners to induce investors to buy the senior securities. By issuing warrants, a corporation can issue senior securities at more favorable interest rates.

The company issuing warrants will eventually dilute its common stock. However, since that event will occur sometime in the future, there is the presumption that a company will be in better financial shape and the dilution will have little effect. Whereas rights are issued to stockholders for immediate capital, warrants are often part of a package of debt financing.

Almost 300 companies have warrants outstanding, and many are detachable and trade in the secondary market. The warrant empowers its holder to buy the shares of a corporation, usually at 15 or 25 percent above the market price. (When warrants are attached to bonds, the surrender of the bonds at par obviates the need to put up cash.)

Warrants have value, especially time value if their expiration date is far in the future. The prices of warrants are kept in line by arbitrageurs who sell them when overpriced and buy them when underpriced. Every warrant has a theoretical value. If, for example, a warrant represents a claim on one share of common stock, at $25 per share, and the stock is currently selling in the market at $30, the warrant has an intrinsic value of $5 (1 × $5). If the price of the warrant falls to $3, the arbitrageur will short the common stock at $30 and buy the warrants.

By exercising the cheap warrant, the speculator will receive $25 shares for a total cost of $28 ($25 plus $3), a net profit of $2 per share. On the other hand, if the warrant rises from its theoretical value of $5 to $7, there is no incentive to exercise. It is unlikely that anyone will pay $32

(the exercise price, $25, plus $7) for $30 shares. A specu-
lator might short the warrants in this case.

The theoretical value of a warrant is determined by the
following formula:

Market price of common stock – Exercise
price × Number of shares per warrant

For example, take the case of Manville Corporation, the
building construction supplier, which has a warrant to
purchase one common stock at $9.40 while the current
market price is $10.50:

$$(\$10.50 - 9.40) \times (1) = \$1.10$$

Though the theoretical value is $1.10, for a while that
warrant was selling at two and three times its theoretical
value. Perhaps the expiration date of June 5, 1996, helped
to lift the price, plus the prospects of Manville putting
bankruptcy and the attendant asbestos problems behind it.

This formula is useful when the current market price is
greater than the exercise price. If the market price is less
than the exercise price, the warrant is valueless, except for
some time value. Such warrants sell for pennies but can be
interesting speculations if there is sufficient time for a
business turnaround.

Since warrants are forms of cheap, long calls on the
underlying shares, they are a favorite of speculators. For
small sums, you can control significant positions. Since the
price appreciates faster than the price of common stock,
warrants provide great leverage if there is no great premium.

Y • O • U • R   M • O• V• E

- Since stock rights enable you to purchase new common stock of a corporation at a subscription or exercise price that is lower than the current market price, it can be profitable for you to buy the rights and subscribe to the new stock. Stock obtained through a rights offering avoids commission fees. Moreover, the shares tend to appreciate after a rights offering.
- Since some rights offerings are met with indifference by the market, it is possible to purchase underpriced rights at the end of an offering.
- Warrants give you a long call option on the underlying common stock. Since they often are issued as a result of a reorganization where the fortunes of a corporation are in doubt, they tend to fluctuate a great deal. Another reason for the fluctuation is the marginal status of warrants: warrant owners have virtually no rights in the corporate structure.
- Warrants are at times underpriced. By analyzing the theoretical value of warrant, it is possible to buy underpriced warrants and exercise them in order to acquire the price difference.
- Warrants give you leverage, enabling you to control far more shares than would otherwise be possible with limited funds.

• 8 •

Speculating Abroad

GREENER GRASS

First the global village, now global speculation. It is inevitable that, as the world is tied more tightly together, the temptation grows to play in someone else's backyard. The last decade has witnessed the dramatic rise of international trade, the spread of multinational corporations and the growth of the Pacific Rim and the newly industrialized countries.

Moreover, the future is no less intriguing as the European Economic Community attempts to integrate its markets by 1992 and eventually popularize a European currency. The democratization of the former Soviet Union and Eastern Europe will open new investment opportunities throughout the 1990s. With the reduction of trade barriers and the end of capital controls, there is a trend toward the unification of financial markets. Many investors and speculators are taking advantage of these opportunities.

There are many ways of speculating abroad. High on the list are the stock and bond markets of countries as familiar as the United Kingdom and as distant as Thailand. Whether by means of direct investment or one of the international mutual funds, the speculator immediately takes on an additional element of risk, that of foreign exchange rates. Whether buying British Airways, Hong Kong Electric, Royal Dutch, Sony, DeBeers or Club Med, the speculator is also buying an exposure to pound sterling, Hong Kong dollars, Dutch guilders, Japanese yen, South African rands or French francs.

These international investments are part of the reason for the growth of the foreign exchange market. Foreign exchange was once a more placid area, with exchange rates fixed by international agreement. Currencies have been freely floating since 1971 (except for the European Economic Community, where currencies are loosely tied in a channel of permissible fluctuations).

Government intervention in these markets is often destabilizing, and it is arguable whether national central banks have sufficient resources to stem or turn a tide in the foreign exchange market. What is not debatable is the enormous attention these markets have attracted in recent years.

The play in the foreign exchange markets is intense, ranging from the actions of treasurers of multinational corporations in the futures markets to tourists in the cash market. Central to most players is the dollar: it represents the American economy and the political and financial commitments of the United States, but it is also the major international reserve currency. It is not the only currency for international trade, but much of that trade is conducted, billed and paid for in dollars.

Finally, there is a small but vocal international constituency that believes that currencies backed by government fiat rather than by hard reserves, such as gold, are subject to inflation and subsequent depreciation. One defense to this problematic condition is to diversify assets into a number of different currencies and/or precious metals. Asset allocation, to this way of thinking, must be global, not just a question of percentages of stocks to bonds.

Consequently, the rise and fall of the dollar and the interest in cross-rates (e.g., the yen-sterling relationship or that of the Swiss franc–German mark) have moved to center stage. The question of what the dollar is worth is now second only to how the market is doing. In the early 1980s the dollar was too strong: by 1985 it crested, and after the Plaza Agreement, central banks attempted to drive it down. The U.S. Treasury succeeded in weakening its own unit of currency to help the export trade and the trade deficit until the dollar bottomed in late 1987. It turned upward in 1990 and 1991, recapturing some of its lost ground. The dollar's value in the last decade has clearly been dictated by political as much as economic forces. Anyone playing in this ball park must keep one eye cocked toward the politics of foreign exchange and the diplomacy of money.

As trade patterns change and as national currencies strengthen and weaken in the eyes of global strategists, the dollar rises and falls. This provides an opportunity for alert speculators to profit from these swings. For example, if you had paid attention to the Plaza Agreement in 1985 and understood the implications of a weaker dollar, you would have sold dollar denominated assets and bought francs, pounds, marks and yen. In the next four years, the dollar fell about 50 percent against these other currencies. Speculating in foreign currencies and foreign assets has been highly profitable in recent years.

CURRENCIES: WHICH MARKET IS BEST?

There are five different ways to speculate in currencies:

1. the spot market
2. the forward market

3. the futures market
4. options on the futures
5. options on the physical currencies

The spot and forward markets need not concern you since the former is an individual cash transaction in currency and the latter is only for institutional investors and banks.

The futures markets in currencies are relatively new, only evolving after currencies became free of government control. Both commercial banks and central banks were initially chary of futures markets in currencies since they would lose both business and control of these lucrative markets. However, with the beginning of free-floating exchange rates, there was no turning back. The value of currencies is now determined by foreign exchange dealers situated around the world, as well as by individual speculators who create, ride and eventually reverse currency trends. It is extraordinarily risky and can be enormously rewarding to some participants.

The International Monetary Market (IMM), a subsidiary of the Chicago Mercantile Exchange, is the center of currency futures trading. Since currency futures are similar to other commodity contracts, they are found on the same page in the financial press.

Currency contracts have fixed sizes and a sequential series of expiration dates. While a forward contract might well be written on any currency, there are only half a dozen or so active currency futures. Table 8.1 shows the most active currency futures, their sizes and the value of a minimum price fluctuation on the IMM.

There are other less active futures contracts, such as the Mexican peso and the French franc.

What makes currency futures so exciting is the large amount of leverage they provide. It is possible to put up as little as $1,500 of initial margin for a pound sterling

TABLE 8.1   The Most Active Currency Futures on the IMM

Unit of Currency	Contract Size	Value of a Tick
British pound	25,000	$12.50
Canadian dollar	100,000	10.00
Japanese yen	12,500,000	6.25
Swiss franc	125,000	6.25
German mark	125,000	6.25

contract that might have a value of $37,500 ($1.50 × 25,000) when the pound is worth $1.50.

Currencies can and do fluctuate widely for a variety of reasons, some of which are unfathomable. If the U.K. chancellor of the exchequer brings in an unexpected budget, the pound may weaken, but it will also fall if an oil rig in the North Sea explodes, reducing the volume of saleable British crude. In brief, there are many reasons for currency changes, and not all of them are obvious. When you are on the right side, you can double your money in short order; and when you are on the wrong side, your principal will vanish just as quickly. A fluctuation of five points (0.05 × 25,000) is $1,250.

Quotations in the daily press for the British pound look like Table 8.2.

The notation in this table is for the September contract. On the next lines will be the December contract, followed by March and as far out as there is interest. This contract was off 2, or $500.

Most currency futures contracts are bought or sold with the understanding that the buyer or seller will never have to make or take delivery. As with other commodity contracts, the contract is terminated through an offsetting transaction. It is possible to take (or make) physical delivery of the foreign currency in question if proper arrange-

TABLE 8.2 British Pound Quotations

Season High	Low	Open Interest	Open	High	Low	Close	Change
1.7754	1.4750	24,853	1.6472	1.6540	1.6382	1.6538	−2

ments are made, but only 1 percent of all currency futures are ended in that way.

As earlier noted, currencies can fluctuate rapidly and widely. There are daily limits (in the case of the pound, $1,250, with similar limits on the other currencies) except in the nearest month contract (closest to expiration) when the move is without limit. Regardless how distant the expiration date, all futures contracts are marked to the market daily. This daily accounting means that you may be required to put up additional maintenance margin to keep your position. If you do not, you will be sold out and forced to take a loss.

HOW RISKY ARE CURRENCY FUTURES?

The accepted wisdom is that currency futures are highly risky. All commodity contracts can show sudden and erratic moves, but the currencies perhaps more than most, especially in periods of economic uncertainty and international confusion. Professional traders suggest that 90 percent of all currency futures do not end up in the profit column. Or to put it another way, the odds against making money are nine to one against you!

As with all options, a currency option gives the buyer of a call or put the right, but not the obligation, to execute a currency futures contract. One would clearly not exercise if it meant an immediate loss. Therefore, the option gives the buyer a predetermined risk—you cannot lose more than the price of the option.

Since currency options are derivative instruments, they follow the trends of the futures. The most popular currency option is the one on the German deutsche mark; it generally has the greatest open interest, with the Japanese yen running a close second. The unification of Germany is likely to see the mark as the dominant European currency throughout the Nineties. Under "Currency Trading," where futures and options are quoted in the press, you will see a typical entry for the mark, as in Table 8.3.

To see how a currency option works, assume that you expected a fall in the price of dollars, or conversely, a rise in the price of deutsche marks. You would buy a call option. If on the other hand, you expected a weaker deutsche mark and a stronger dollar, you should consider buying puts.

In Table 8.3, a $.50 strike price for the September call quoted at 4.18 must be read as $.00418 per deutsche mark. This 4.18 quote represents a premium of $523 ($.00418 × 125,000). Thus, the premium of $523 enables a call option buyer to receive a futures contract if the value of that contract rises. While you might take delivery of the futures contract, most traders will simply sell the option at a higher price to realize a profit. If the price of the contract declines, the price of the premium will also decline. Upon the expiration date, if the price of the futures contract is below the exercise price of the call, you lose the entire investment in the option.

TABLE 8.3 Typical Entry for the Deutsche Mark

Strike Price	Calls			Puts		
	Aug.	Sep.	Oct.	Aug.	Sep.	Oct.
4900	5.18	5.18	no op	no tr	0.02	0.03
5000	4.18	4.18	no op	no tr	0.04	0.06
5100	3.18	3.23	no tr	0.01	0.07	0.13

As with other options, the price of the option depends on whether the option is in the money, at the money or out of the money.

- An in-the-money option is one in which the exercise price of the call is lower than the price of the futures.
- An at-the-money option indicates that the exercise price of the call is at or near the price of the futures.
- An out-of-the money option shows the exercise price of the call is higher than the price of the futures.

In Table 8.3, the call enables the buyer to take possession of a September $.50 futures contract. If the contract was selling at $.49, the option would have no intrinsic value. At $.50 it begins to develop intrinsic value, but it still must overcome the option premium of $523 to be worthwhile. Since every one-cent move equals $1,250, the future must move slightly more than 2/5ths ($500) of one cent to become profitable. The September futures were then selling at .5418; therefore, the option was in the money, that is, the exercise price of the call was lower than the price of the futures.

Because the call was in the money, it was relatively costly, and it presents the buyer with the least leverage. On the other extreme is the out-of-the-money call. That premium is the cheapest (which also means that it entails the least risk in the outlay of money) since the price reflects no intrinsic value, only time value.

Buying puts can be profitable if the deutsche mark has a substantial decline. The put option allows a speculator to sell a futures contract at the strike price. Therefore, a decline in the value of the deutsche mark will increase the value of the option. A trader's profit will be based on the amount that the futures contract's price has declined below the put's strike price, less the premium paid for the put in the first place.

SELLING OPTIONS

Speculators can sell calls and puts on foreign currency futures contracts. However, selling naked calls leaves you open to the twists of the market. When you sell a call on a futures contract that you do not own, you receive a premium. But you also take on the obligation to sell one futures contract at a fixed strike price if the option is exercised. This obligation can be terminated at any time by buying a call identical to one that was initially sold.

Call writers assume that the market will either fall or be static. The premiums received are then all profit if that holds true. The speculator is betting that the time value of the option will lose its value before an exercise is worthwhile. If a September 50 call is sold at 1 with the futures at .4800, the call expires worthlessly if the futures are at or below .5000. On the other hand, if the futures moved to .5050, the option would sell for 0.5 on expiration—a profit, but a smaller one. If the futures moved higher, the trader would be forced to buy back the option at a higher price and take a loss. The break-even point is the exercise price of the call, plus the premium received—in this case 51.

It is also possible to speculate through put selling. When a put is written, you are granting the purchaser the right to deliver a futures contract to you at the strike price at any time until the option expires. Naked put writing is not quite as speculative as naked call writing: a call has no ceiling in a strong up move, but puts can only go to zero in a downdraft. There is more room on the upside than on the downside. The call writer profits if the futures remain below the strike price, but the put writer profits at any price above the strike price.

The put writer must be aware of the break-even point: the exercise price of the put minus the premium received. If the price of the futures drops somewhat below the exercise price of the put, there is not much likelihood of an exercise if there is a lot of time value left.

If there is not much time left and the futures price declines sharply below the exercise price so that it is in the money, it is likely to be exercised. If the trader does not close out the position before an exercise of the option, the exercise results in a long futures position. When you take on a futures position you not only have an open exposure, but are obliged to put up margin money as well.

It is precisely the limiting of exposure while maintaining the speculative characteristics of the futures that is so desirable in the option on the futures. The option gives you staying power! You may be right on the general direction of the currency, but a sudden break if you are using stops will sell you out of the futures. With the option on the futures contract, you can comfortably sit out the temporary retracement and wait for the trend to resume.

OPTIONS ON THE PHYSICALS

The final market for anyone wishing to speculate in foreign exchange is the Philadelphia Stock Exchange, where exchange-traded currency options are traded. These are options on the actual spot currencies, rather than options on futures contracts. Therefore, the option buyer obtains a right (but not an obligation) by paying the premium to buy the currency if the option is exercised, or conversely, he or she can sell the currency if the option is a put. And the same is true if you are an option seller: you are obliged to sell the foreign currency at a fixed price in dollars if a call is exercised, or to buy the foreign currency at a fixed price if a put is exercised.

These currency options differ from the options on currency futures in another way: they are half the size of the corresponding futures contracts traded on the IMM. This is of great benefit to the speculator with limited resources. The option contract sizes are as follows:

Currency	Contract Size
British pounds	31,250
Canadian dollars	50,000
German marks	62,500
Japanese yen	6,250,000
Swiss francs	62,500

The premiums are calculated in a similar fashion, except that the size of the contract virtually reduces the premium in half. Therefore, when the option on British pounds is 2.85, the premium is $891 (0.0285 × 31,250), compared with the option on the pound futures, which would be $1,781 (0.0285 × 62,500).

All the strategies available to options on the futures apply to these currency options. You can use these currency options, instead of using options on the futures, as a form of speculating or as insurance on the currency futures. Thus, if a futures contract is quite profitable, you can purchase two options on the same foreign currency to lock in the profit without disturbing the futures position.

For example, your deutsche mark futures contract rose from 46 to 50, a 4-cent profit that translates into $5,000 (0.04 × 125,000). Since there are still a few months before expiration, with additional potential gain, you buy two put options at 50 for $500 each, or a total of $1,000. If the futures fall, the puts will gain in value, offsetting the decline. This strategy costs $1,000, and it lowers the net profit to $4,000. However, if the futures contract keeps appreciating, each cent the contract advances means an additional gain of $1,250.

Of course, the puts could be bought naked, that is, without the benefit of having a long futures position. This is a simple bear strategy speculation. A similar bearish stance suggests that a trader sell uncovered calls. In this case, the writer is exposed to potentially unlimited loss if the underlying currency increases in value. However, the premium income will go some way to cushion the loss.

A bullish trader can write uncovered put options. While the currency remains at or above the exercise price of the put, the option will not be exercised. The income from selling such options can be considerable, allowing for great leverage on the initial margin money. There is danger in writing naked or uncovered calls, but the return on investment for those who can withstand the stress is highly profitable.

Y·O·U·R   M·O·V·E

- Consider speculating abroad, but remember that you take on additional risk in the fluctuations of foreign exchange rates.
- Foreign mutual funds attracted a great deal of attention with the overthrow of communism in Eastern Europe. Subsequently, they were bid up far in excess of their net asset value. If you wish to speculate in foreign funds, do not pay much more than what they are worth.
- It is less costly to buy foreign shares that are traded in the U.S. markets in the form of American Depository Receipts (ADRs).
- To speculate in the foreign exchange market, you must decide whether you wish to deal in the futures, options on the futures or options on the physical currencies. First start with the options on the physical currencies since the size of the contract is less intimidating. Once you are familiar with that, you might try options on the futures. If you are not averse to great risk, the futures

markets provide the greatest volatility for the least money.
- Selling naked options on the futures is extremely risky, but the premium income will soften the blow if the market moves against you.

S • H • O • R • T • C • U • T

International Mutual Funds

- Alliance International
- Fidelity Europe
- GT Pacific Growth
- Ivy International
- Scudder Global
- T. Rowe Price International Stock

• 9 •

A Note on Speculating and Swindles

Speculators are perhaps more vulnerable to swindles and scams than investors since they welcome risk rather than avoiding it. They are quick to act (sometimes too quick), for that is the nature of the markets in which they deal. The French would say that it is a *deformation professionnel,* a professional weakness. Therefore, it is critical to be aware not only of the latest schemes to part you from your money but also of the questions to ask to avoid being fleeced by fly-by-night operators.

To be sure, there are numerous white-collar criminals that try to separate investors from their cash. The public lost over $450 million in five years. The actual figure exceeds that figure since this survey by the North American Securities Administrators and the Council of Better Business Bureaus counted only scams where investors' losses were greater than $500,000.

There are regulatory safeguards and self-policing by the exchanges, and you can resort to the law courts if you can find and apprehend the "dirty, rotten scoundrels." But the best precautions are to be aware of current scams.

Common sense is your best line of defense. If it sounds too good to be true, it probably is not true. The problems often arise from confidence men (and women) who frequently come cloaked with an aura of authority or are associated with bona fide organizations. Such organizations know nothing of the individual's nefarious activities and have not authorized or sanctioned his or her schemes. However, the association with such an organization, real or alleged, is often enough to overcome one's normal or natural defenses.

Telemarketing is the swindler's method of choice because it's cheap, easy, automated and impersonal. Of late, religious scams are pandemic. The telemarketer poses as a member of a particular church, "your church," in an attempt to gain trust. Born-again Christian financial planners seem to flourish these days, but no sect is immune from the scam artist. They persuade victims that their religious connection can be relied on, and some even go so far as to suggest that the "investment" is divinely inspired. Many vulnerable victims have lost their life savings to these con men.

Religion is the soft sell, while gold is the hard sell of telemarketing. Whenever the price of gold makes a new yearly high, the dirt-pile scam flourishes. The voice on the other end of the line attempts to convince the listener that there are riches in the tailings (the mine waste) and claims that his or her company has the secret process to withdraw the gold.

Other swindlers will try to persuade you that you can store gold (or silver or platinum) in a bank for 10 percent down. Since the metal is your collateral, all you have to do is pay back the loan while waiting for a price rise to provide a great profit on your leveraged position. It sounds good, but the price gain would have to be rather exceptional to cover your interest, commissions and storage fees. And some telemarketers simply take the money and run.

Penny stocks are often manipulated by the unscrupulous. Even though the majority may sell between $1 and $5, there are some worthwhile issues among these cheap issues. But you must do your homework since so many of them are fraudulently promoted. Not only must you do some research to see that a company is something more than a corporate shell, but you should investigate to see who makes a market in the issue. Sound companies usually have a number of market makers, but the dubious outfits have only one.

Fraud in the futures market is no less persistent. One common technique is to hook people by being the infallible forecaster. The con artist first calls with a well-researched tip as to the direction of the particular market—it makes no difference which one. No, he's not inviting you to invest since you shouldn't do that with anyone you don't know. The con artist then calls back a few weeks later since, lo and behold, the market acted precisely the way he or she predicted. Your appetite is now whetted—and more so, since on the second call you are offered another well-researched tip. A few weeks later there is a third call, and, of course, the prophecy was fulfilled. By this time, the victim is eager and willing to commit good funds and perhaps a little more money to make up for the missed opportunities. The infallibility comes from a long list of calls: half are wrong the first time, and that leaves a pool of potential clients from the other half. All things being equal, the con artist loses half on the second call. This leaves an infallible record with 25 percent of his or her original list. The laws of chance and gullibility are on the con artist's side.

WHAT QUESTIONS SHOULD YOU ASK?

To avoid swindles, the National Futures Association has prepared a list of suggestions that will turn off most swindlers. They are not foolproof since human greed is easily aroused and difficult to control. But they are worth considering when you are faced with a cold call from someone. After all, telemarketing is a respectable way to do business, and many companies and brokerage houses use this method. It is up to you to separate the good from the bad. The recommended questions are as follows:

1. Where did you get my name? Computer-generated lists are available for almost any purpose. If you have ever been the victim of a scam, your name will circulate for years.
2. What risks are involved? Any assurance that there is no risk, outside of government securities, is clearly misleading.
3. Can you send literature? Either it's too hot a deal to wait for the mails, or the promised information never arrives.
4. Can I show your proposal to my accountant, banker and other advisers? What's the matter? Can't you make your own decisions? Trying to shame you into a decision is a ploy almost as powerful as greed.
5. Can I have the names of the firm's principals? If it sounds like you might check up on the information, you might be more trouble than you're worth.
6. Can you provide references? The names may be phony, but there should be either someone you know or an organization with a reputation that will vouch for previous dealings.
7. Do you have any risk disclosure documents? These are required in most investment areas, especially in securities, options and futures. Moreover, in the ordinary course of business, you are required to read, understand and sign the prospectus and other documents.
8. Are the investments traded on a regular exchange? Not all bona fide investments are, but if you do your speculating on such an exchange, there is less likelihood of being hoodwinked.
9. What regulatory agencies supervise your firm? Unless state and federal agencies are supervising, think twice

about any involvement. Should there be problems, to whom do you complain?

10. How long has your company been in business? Some new investments may be the best investments, but you will sleep better if you know that the business has been around for a number of years.

11. What's your track record? A reputable firm should be able to show you a documented performance record. But past performance is no guarantee of future performance.

12. When and where can I meet with you? Most scam artists will not take the time. Moreover, boiler-room operators have no intention of inviting you to their quarters.

13. Where, exactly, will my money be? If your funds will be commingled rather than segregated, who will provide an accounting? Registered investment firms maintain separate accounts for all their clients.

14. How much of my money will go for commissions and fees? This should be spelled out and not brushed aside with an evasive "what's really important is how much money you are going to make." Find out if there are any carrying charges.

15. How can I liquidate and when will the proceeds be returned? Not all good investments can be liquidated easily, such as a real estate partnership. You should also find out if there are any costs attached to ending your investment.

16. If disputes arise, how are they resolved? Find out if the business or regulatory organization makes use of arbitration or would be amenable to some sort of reparations procedure.

The above questions were adapted from the National Futures Association pamphlet, "Investment Swindles: How They Work and How To Avoid Them."

Finally, if you do make an investment and/or a speculation, make sure that you receive a prompt and accurate accounting of your funds. No one can guarantee that you will make money on any investment. However, if you can avoid the con artists and the scams, you will certainly have a far better chance.

Glossary

arbitrage The simultaneous buying and selling of the identical item in different markets to profit from slight price differentials.

at the money The exercise price of an option is equal to the price of its underlying shares.

beta A mathematic measurement of a stock's sensitivity to the movement of the general market. A beta of 1 means that the stock moves in line with the market, but a beta of 1.5 means that it is 50 percent more volatile on the upside than the general market.

buy-write strategy A technique of buying a common stock and selling an option against it for the premium income.

calls A call option gives the buyer the right to buy 100 shares of the underlying stock at a stated price at any time before the option expires.

cash account An account where all transactions are for cash.

commission merchant A broker or agent who deals only in commodities.

convertible bond A bond that gives its holder the privilege of exchanging it for common stock of the issuing corporation on a preferred basis at some later date.

deep discount bond A bond that is either issued far below its face value or one that has fallen because of the financial difficulties of the issuer.

exercise price The set price for which shares can be purchased or sold in an option contract. It is also referred to as the strike price.

ex-rights   The stock is sold without the rights attached.

flat   Bonds that are in default are traded flat, that is, no accrual of interest is added to the sale price of the bonds or deducted from the purchase price.

initial margin   The amount of money required to establish a margin account. This figure is set by the Federal Reserve System.

in the money   A call is in the money when the underlying shares are selling above the exercise price. A put is in the money when the underlying shares are selling below the strike price.

intrinsic value   That portion of an option's value attributable to its selling in the money. In a call, it is the excess of the market price of the underlying shares over the strike price; in a put, it is the excess of the strike price of the option over the market value of the underlying shares.

junk bond   High-yielding bonds that do not have investment ratings—they are rated lower than BBB by some rating agencies.

leverage   The relationship of corporate debt to equity can affect earnings when a significant amount of earnings must be paid to service bond interest or preferred stock dividends. If a corporation earns a return on the borrowed money above the cost of the debt, the leverage is successful. This will increase the return on the common stock without additional investment. If the leverage is unsuccessful, it will decimate earnings and leave little if anything to the stockholder. The use of credit in a margin account is a form of leverage.

long hedge   The purchase of a futures contract as a hedge against the sale of a cash commodity.

long position   This describes the ownership of common stock in the anticipation of an increase in price.

maintenance margin   The amount of money required by a futures firm to hold a futures position.

margin   The use of a brokerage firm's credit to purchase securities. For the accommodation, the broker charges interest.

marginable securities   All securities listed on the national stock exchanges plus many that are traded in the over-the-counter (OTC) market.

margin call   The demand by a brokerage firm for additional funds (or marginable securities) when a customer's equity declines below a minimum standard.

marked to the market   The daily tally of a futures account in order to determine if there are sufficient funds in the account either to avoid a margin call or to make a new commitment.

market multiple   The average price-earnings ratio of a general index.

naked   The selling of call options for the premium income without owning the securities. Trading naked in put options is equally dangerous—you may not have the funds available if the put option is exercised.

option   A right sold by one party to another for a premium to buy (a call option) or sell (a put option) a security at a fixed price during a specific period of time.

out of the money   A condition in which the strike price is above the market price of the underlying shares for a call; in a put, the strike price is below the market price of the underlying shares.

premium   The cost for transacting an option agreement.

put   An option to sell a security at a fixed price during a stated period of time.

right   A subscription privilege to the holder of common stock to buy additional shares in a corporation at a fixed price.

short hedge   The sale of a futures contract to offset the holding of a cash commodity.

spread   Two options, a put and a call, on the same stock and expiring on the same day. However, the strike price on the two options is different, and the speculator hopes to profit from the change in the difference. By buying the put, the speculator is guaranteed a sale if the market drops but is also guaranteed a buy if the market advances.

straddle   This similar to a spread, but the strike price of the two options is identical.

strike price   *See* exercise price.

time value   The value of an option premium that reflects only the period to expiration. Sometimes this is called the extrinsic value.

warrants   A certificate giving the holder a right to purchase common stock of a corporation at a fixed price within a specified period of time. Warrants are usually issued with debt issues as an enticement to buy the senior securities.

when issued   This indicates that a transaction is based on the actual issuance of the security. It is a conditional transaction to be settled only if the security is indeed issued.

Index